CONQUERING
CHILDHOOD
ASTHMA

An Illustrated Guide to Understanding the Treatment
and Control of Childhood Asthma

Bruce K. Rubin, MD

Michael T. Newhouse, MD

Peter J. Barnes, DM

1998
Empowering Press, Hamilton, Canada

Canadian Cataloguing in Publication Data

Rubin, Bruce K.
   Conquering childhood asthma.

Includes index.
ISBN 1-896998-02-X

1. Asthma in children — Popular works. I. Barnes, Peter J., 1946–
II. Newhouse, Michael T. III. Title

RJ436.A8R82 1997   618.92'238   C97-932192-1

For distribution information contact the publisher:

Empowering Press

4 Hughson Street South, P.O. Box 620, L.C.D. 1
Hamilton, Ontario, Canada L8N 3K7
Tel: 905-522-7017; Fax: 905-522-7839;
e-mail: info@bcdecker.com

The authors and publisher have made every effort to ensure that the patient care recommended herein, including choice of drugs and drug dosages, is in accord with the accepted standards and practice at the time of publication. However, since research and regulation constantly change clinical standards, the reader is urged to check the product information sheet included in the package of each drug, which includes recommended doses, warnings, and contraindications. This is particularly important with new or infrequently used drugs. Any treatment regimen, particularly one involving medication, involves inherent risk that must be weighed on a case-by-case basis against the benefits anticipated. The reader is cautioned that the purpose of this book is to inform and enlighten; the information contained herein is not intended as, and should not be employed as, a substitute for individual diagnosis and treatment.

Printed in Canada

CONTENTS

You are likely reading this book because you or your child has asthma and you want to know more about this disease. You want answers to any number of questions.

What is asthma? What causes it? How does the doctor know it is asthma? Is it inherited? Is it caused by allergies? Can it be cured? If not, can it be controlled? Can my child lead a normal life?

We wrote this book to provide the answers to these and other questions asked many times by our young asthmatic patients and their parents. We also wrote it because we believe that you and your child can do a great deal to conquer asthma and maintain good health. Ninety-five percent of all asthmatics now lead normal, active lives at work and at play. Indeed, many successful Olympic athletes are asthmatics!

This book will help you and your child understand more about asthma. You will learn how to treat and control the disease, how to monitor it day by day, and how to judge if your child's condition is stable. If your child's asthma is getting worse, you will know what to do before symptoms become serious enough to mean a dash to the hospital. We believe that this book will give you and your child the confidence to care for the condition and so to avoid most major flare-ups. With this book and intermittent follow–up with your doctor and other care-givers it should be possible for you to conquer childhood asthma.

Bruce K. Rubin, MD
Michael T. Newhouse, MD
Peter J. Barnes, DM

CHAPTER ONE

WHAT IS ASTHMA?
IS IT BECOMING MORE COMMON?

Asthma is by far the most common chronic childhood disease, and it occurs all over the world, particularly in industrialized countries. Asthma is more common in boys. One in six children will have asthma at some time in their life. The condition causes more school absenteeism and more emergency department visits than any other childhood illness.

Asthma is a name that came to us from the ancient Greeks, who applied it to a group of conditions whose main features were shortness of breath, cough, wheeze, and chest tightness. In children, asthma is sometimes called by other names such as "wheezy bronchitis" or "reactive airways disease." To keep things as clear as possible, we will only use the term "asthma."

Figure 1–1. Composite diagram showing the various associations between asthma and tobacco smoke, infection, acid regurgitation, sinusitis, and night-time.

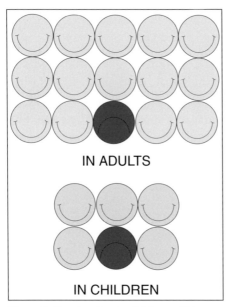

IN ADULTS

IN CHILDREN

Figure 1–2. One in six children will have asthma symptoms at some time during childhood.

Asthma involves an excessive narrowing of the air passages. The narrowing is due to the bronchial muscle that surrounds the walls of the air passages, swelling of the airway lining, and an excessive production of mucus. This combination of responses is called *inflammation*, and it can be caused by allergies to things like cats, pollens, molds, and house dust mites. Allergies are not the only problem, however. Asthma is commonly triggered by viral infections in children or adults. It may also be triggered by exposure to chemicals, especially when adults are exposed to these at work. Once asthma is established, the airways become hyperreactive or "twitchy," and further exposure can cause them to narrow.

Although asthma cannot be "cured," it can, and should, be kept under control by use of anti-inflammatory medications, which *prevent* or control the inflammation. This is better than simply using medications to relieve the symptoms when they occur. The approach is similar to preventing sunburn with a sun block, rather than treating the painful and irritable skin with pain relievers and creams.

Because safe and effective anti-inflammatory medications are now available to control asthma, the need to use bronchodilator (reliever) medications, which provide only short-term relief, has been greatly decreased.

Surveys indicate that asthma is becoming more common. The number of asthmatic children in Australia and New Zealand has doubled during the past 20 years. Twice as many people in England are being treated for asthma as was the case 10 years ago. More people are having more severe attacks, and not surprisingly, hospitalization rates have also increased. The cause of this increase is not known, although some experts believe that it could be due to greater numbers of allergens, such as house dust mites in homes that are warmer, more tightly sealed, and better humidified.

Research has suggested that eating diets high in salt or animal fats may contribute to airway inflammation. It is interesting that asthma is very rare among the Inuit (Eskimo) who live on a diet of fish, in remote communities where few pollutants or pollens are present. Recent studies suggest that industrial pollution usually does not *initiate* asthma, although it can cause airway injury. This is especially true when pollutant levels are very high due to thermal inversions in the spring, summer, and fall, which can result in flare-ups of asthma.

THE NORMAL AIR PASSAGES AND LUNGS: HOW INJURY LEADS TO ASTHMA

The lungs are two large air-filled organs inside the chest, one on each side of the heart. Each lung is like a sponge consisting of air passages that branch like a tree from the windpipe (trachea) to the smallest airways (bronchioles) that terminate in air sacs (alveoli). Air first passes through the nose or mouth where it is humidified and cleared of particles and most irritant gases. Each lung contains about 150 million alveoli, each of which is about the size of the head of a pin.

The large air passages are prevented from collapsing by rings of cartilage and the smaller ones within the lungs are held open by the tethering action of the air sacs that sur-

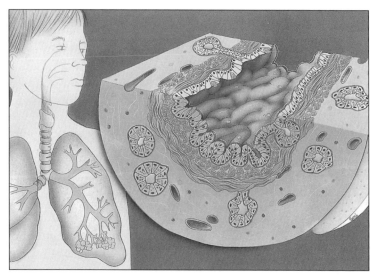

Figure 2–1. *Left:* The normal air passages from the nose and mouth join at the voice-box (larynx) which is attached to the windpipe (trachea). The trachea branches again and again within each lung. The branches (bronchi and bronchioles) end in the air sacs (alveoli). *Right:* Cross-section (three-dimensional) of a normal airway cut in half showing: in the center, smooth muscle layer and blood vessels and near the outer edge, mucous glands (circular structures).

round the airways. These act like elastic bands pulling on the walls of the air passages. Each alveolus consists of a very thin membrane. This membrane separates the air space from the blood space. When we breathe, the air is carried into the air sacs. Because of the huge surface area of the lungs (the size of a tennis court if it were stretched out in a flat sheet) the oxygen rapidly passes into the red blood cells to be carried to every tissue cell in the body via the bloodstream. At the same time as oxygen passes into the blood, one of the important waste products of the body's cells, a gas called carbon dioxide, is rapidly discharged from the blood into the air sacs and then exhaled. Healthy children breathe 10 to 15 times each minute (infants up to 20 times each minute) and faster when more oxygen is needed, such as during exercise. Sensors in the bloodstream and brain are continuously stimulated by carbon dioxide levels and automatically control the rate and depth of breathing so that the body gets the amount of oxygen it needs and disposes of the *excess* carbon dioxide.

The bellows-like pump that drives the air into and out of the lungs consists of muscles between the ribs of the chest wall and the diaphragm, a large flat muscle that completely closes the space between the chest and the abdomen. The red blood cells are pumped through the blood vessels in the lungs and then to the tissue cells all over the body.

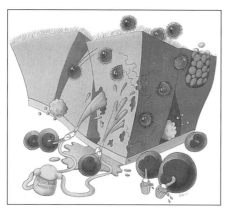

Figure 2–2. Mediators from inflammatory cells can cause even more damage to the airway.

THE AIR PASSAGES

The air passages start at the nose and end in

the alveoli. They are lined by a surface layer consisting of ciliated and goblet cells, and mucous glands. The goblet cells and mucous glands produce the protective surface layer of mucus. Below the mucus is a thin watery liquid (periciliary fluid) in which the microscopic hair-like cilia beat at

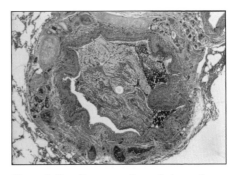

Figure 2–3. Cross section of airway in fatal asthma with airway swollen and blocked with mucus.

1000 times a minute to move the mucus quickly towards the throat where it is swallowed. The mucus traps foreign particles and bacteria that are breathed in, and in this way, the air passages are kept clean and sterile. In conditions like cystic fibrosis, the mucus cannot be readily cleared, and these children have ongoing infections of their air passages. Another method for getting rid of excessive mucus is cough. Cough acts as a back-up system should the secretions become excessive or should the cilia become injured by infections or function abnormally.

Beneath these layers is a crisscross layer of muscle that normally acts to narrow the air passages when (healthy) people inhale irritants. However, in asthma, the narrowing of the air passages is much greater than normal, partly because asthmatics have narrower air passages due to swelling of the lining and mucus plugging and because their air passages more readily develop spasm of the muscles in their walls due to airway inflammation.

THE NOSE

Healthy people normally breathe through the nose which warms and humidifies the air and filters out large particles. The nose has a lining very similar to the air passages of the lungs (except for the muscle layer). When you get a cold or an allergic reaction, the lining of the nose swells and forms mucus, resulting in a "runny-nose," which is due to inflammation of the lining of the nose (doctors call this "rhinitis"). The lining also contains nerves, and when these are irritated, sneezing occurs. These features are most commonly seen in "hay fever," along with itchy, runny eyes (conjunctivitis).

HOW DAMAGE TO THE AIRWAYS LEADS TO ASTHMA

Since nonasthmatics exposed to the same allergens or irritants do not develop inflammation of their air passages, doctors do not yet know what actually causes asthma. In some people, asthma is related to allergy. Certain viruses, particularly one called Respitory Syncytial Virus (RSV); certain chemicals in very small concentrations (e.g., toluene diisocyanate and platinum salts); and other gases, such as chlorine

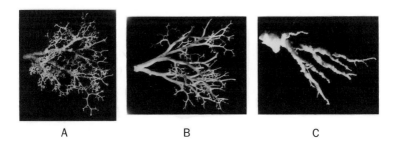

A   B   C

Figure 2–4. Cast of the inside of the airway in asthma. *A)* normal airway; *B)* airway of a person with stable asthma; *C)* airway of a person dying of asthma. There is progressive loss of airway branching due to obstruction.

or ammonia released in *very large* concentrations during chemical spills, can also cause airway injury that leads to asthma.

Allergy is an excessive sensitivity to some of the natural protein or chemical substances present in the air we breathe or the food we eat. If they provoke an excessive reaction of a person's immune system, these substances are considered allergens. The immune system of allergic people seems to over-react to these naturally occurring substances by producing extra antibodies which try to "fight off" the allergen. The reaction is similar to the one mounted against some parasites, such as worms. People can react differently to allergens. Some get hay fever and others skin eczema, eye irritation, or asthma. Some react with a combination of several of these.

Doctors often use skin prick tests to confirm the role of allergens. When tested for a large number of allergens, about one in three completely normal individuals show some skin reactions. The most common reaction takes the form of an itchy hive, which is surrounded by an area of redness. The size of this "wheal" depends on the amount of antibody in the tissue that reacts to a standard "dose" of antigen in the skin test serum. Except in toddlers, these tests are usually used to identify allergens you inhale rather than those in the food you eat. Skin testing is, however, not a very good way to diagnose food allergy in older children and adults, and in children under the age of 2 or 3, skin testing may not be as useful as in older children. This is why a negative skin test may not completely exclude an allergy to a given substance.

CHAPTER THREE

HOW TO TELL IF YOUR CHILD HAS ASTHMA

The typical symptoms of an asthma attack are cough, wheezing, and breathing difficulty. In some infants and children cough can be the only symptom. Most children also have chest tightness, and breathlessness. Often the nose is congested also. These symptoms are fairly easy to identify in older children and adolescents, but in infants and young children, the same symptoms may not mean asthma. The younger child with similar symptoms may only have a viral infection of the air passages. If the smaller air passages are mainly involved, the result can be bronchiolitis, or if the problem is mainly around the voice box or larynx, croup. Sometimes these nonasthmatic conditions respond to anti-inflammatory treatment similar to that used in asthma, and the viruses that cause these conditions may predispose the child to asthma.

Some asthmatic children, especially older ones, may cough and wheeze while younger infants and toddlers may only cough. Breathlessness is common, and some children find breathing easier on sitting up. Asthma symptoms are usually worse at night and in the early morning, with exercise, or exposure to cold air. Laughing and crying can also trigger asthma. Between attacks, most children have few symptoms. If asthma is brought on specifically by allergens such as pollens, symptoms will be worse during the spring, summer, or fall pollen seasons; the symptoms may lessen in winter.

Your child may be asthmatic if (s)he wakes up coughing at night, sometimes to the point of retching and vomiting; appears to be cranky and tired all day; and/or suffers spells of coughing after running, playing vigorously, laughing, or crying. If a child is sent home from school because of constant coughing that disrupts the class, this may be an indication that your child may have asthma, especially if it happens every few weeks. Up to age 5 or 6, a diagnosis of asthma can be difficult to make. Young children attending day-care or kindergarten for the first time often get recurring viral infections.

Not only can viral illnesses be accompanied by similar symptoms without the child having asthma, but also viruses frequently trigger asthma attacks. You should suspect asthma if recurrent and persistent "colds" with cough follow one after the other every 2 or 3 weeks and appear to drag on for more than the expected week or 10 days.

Reflux of stomach contents is common in newborns and infants. This is why infants are usually "burped" when they are fed. Whenever an infant falls asleep with a bottle in its mouth, milk or juice may be regurgitated into the trachea and lungs. For this reason, infants should *never* be put to bed with a bottle. Sometimes bronchitis due to stomach acid regurgitation can coexist with asthma. This makes the diagnosis of asthma particularly difficult since treating only one or the other will not result in full improvement.

Cough can persist for many weeks or months in children with whooping cough (pertussis), with postnasal drip due to sinus infection, or with a congested, runny nose. With conditions that cause postnasal drip, the cough is particularly severe when the child lies down. Also, if a foreign object, such as a plastic toy or peanut, is inhaled, the result may be persistent cough or recurring pneumonia.

As you can see, it may take an expert to sort all this out, make a complete diagnosis, and deal with *all* of the problems, to achieve asthma control.

INFECTION OR ASTHMA?

When children with suspected asthma are first seen by a lung specialist, allergist, or pediatrician, they have often been on repeated courses of antibiotics for "infections," but generally the response has been poor. It is useful to know that children with asthma can cough up yellow phlegm and this does not necessarily indicate infection. This is because the main inflammatory cells in this condition are eosinophils (so called because they contain granules that take up the red chemical stain called eosin), and they give the phlegm its characteristic yellow appearance. If the phlegm of people with asthma is examined with a microscope, many eosinophils are seen. This finding is not present in infections like pneumonia.

The common cold virus is one of the most important triggers of asthma attacks in children. Nearly 70% of patients under the age of 6 years start off an asthma attack with bronchitis, a head cold, or a sinus infection. Think of asthma whenever a head or chest cold in your child seems to always go on for more than 10–14 days. Effective asthma treatment to maintain control, which has been continued for several months, will help to differentiate between asthma and other conditions.

In summary, a single wheezy episode with a viral chest cold does *not* necessarily signify that your child has asthma. Many viral infections cause a transient asthma-like condition, but this usually clears up within a few weeks, or at the most in a month or two. It is *recurring* or *persisting* cough, breathlessness and/or wheezing, often with failure to improve completely between episodes, that are the cardinal features of asthma. The diagnosis of asthma can best be made with certainty over a period of time, by making measurements of lung function, examination of phlegm for eosinophils and assessing response to asthma therapy.

TESTING FOR ASTHMA

The history of the illness that you provide to the doctor is the most important part of making a diagnosis of asthma. At the time of the visit, your child will be assessed for signs of asthma such as nasal congestion or wheezing. We have mentioned that the diagnosis of asthma can sometimes be difficult, since both the history and the findings on physical examination can be present in other conditions as well. A good response to asthma treatment strongly supports the diagnosis of asthma, whereas failure to respond to adequate doses of anti-inflammatory medication suggests that the problem is not asthma, or that asthma is not the only cause of your child's symptoms.

In children over 5 or 6, doctors can test for asthma with simple and painless breathing tests. These tests consist of blowing out as quickly and as completely as possible into a computer, which calculates the total volume of air exhaled and the rate of its exhalation. Airflow rates, referred to as peak expiratory flow (PEF) or forced expiratory volume in one second (FEV_1), are generally reduced in asthma, if symptoms are present at the time the test is done. When asthmatics are symptom-free, however, these test results can be normal. In such cases, children over the age of 4 can be

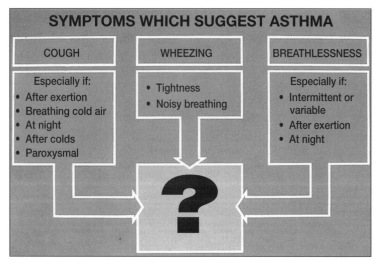

Figure 3–1. Symptoms that suggest asthma.

provided with a simple device called a peak flow meter to take away with them so that measurements can be made daily for several weeks or months until the asthma is stable. In children with severe or variable asthma, PEF may be measured twice daily for a set period. The child's doctor can then adjust the treatment according to the results rather than from symptoms alone. Peak flow measurements and the FEV_1 are discussed in more detail in Chapter 7. Additional tests used to make a diagnosis of asthma and exclude other causes of cough and wheezing include allergy skin testing, exercise or methacholine challenge, and sweat testing to evaluate for cystic fibrosis. Stomach x-rays and night time acid reflux monitoring in the esophagus may be used to evaluate for reflux-related bronchitis. Sometimes, bronchoscopy, which is an examination of the inside of the voice box, wind pipe, and larger air passages using a long, narrow, flexible tube, allows the surface of the air passages to be seen and samples to be taken if necessary. For this procedure, your child will be lightly anaesthetized. Another test, oxygen saturation, is done to ensure that a normal amount of oxygen is getting into your child's blood. In this test, a small probe is attached to the finger tip or ear lobe with a clip. Eosinophils in the phlegm provide strong evidence of asthma.

ASTHMA TRIGGERS

Asthma is almost never triggered by just one exposure to a particular allergen. An attack is usually caused by a combination of exposures to several allergens and triggers, or by a massive exposure to allergens (such as cat dander) after the initial sensitization has taken place. Each additional exposure increases the chances of an attack, and, unless treated, each subsequent episode tends to be more severe.

You can begin to conquer your child's asthma by discovering these triggers and helping your child to avoid them.

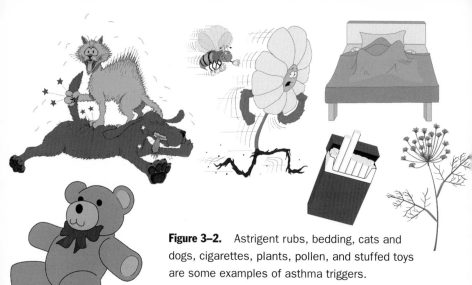

Figure 3–2. Astrigent rubs, bedding, cats and dogs, cigarettes, plants, pollen, and stuffed toys are some examples of asthma triggers.

Your search is likely to be successful if you focus on places where your child is most likely to be exposed. For example, the bedroom, the family car (no smoking there *ever*), or the den or recreation room. Consider such things as feather pillows or comforters, house dust mites that live in pillows, mattresses, shaggy rugs, and stuffed toys, as well as domestic pets, particularly cats and dogs. Also, avoid high humidity and astringent rubs. Keep a diary of symptoms and see if you can relate them to any particular season or exposure, which would suggest pollen or mold sensitivity. Give your doctor as much of this kind of information as possible. This type of information is very valuable in finding the probable causes of your child's asthma, and should lead to effective measures to reduce exposure to these allergens to an absolute minimum.

Flare-ups of asthma are often caused by viral "colds" or pneumonia, especially if the asthma has not been well controlled. Bacterial infections may follow viral infections, and your child may require antibiotics as well as increased asthma treatment. Remember that repeated treatment of "bronchitis" with antibiotics without much effect should make you think of the possibility of asthma!

ALLERGENS AND ALLERGIES

Allergen is the name given to a substance that has made an individual hypersensitive so that, when they are exposed to it again, an excessive inflammatory reaction occurs. The excessive reaction of the body to an allergen is called "allergy." Asthma in children is frequently, but not always, an allergic reaction. Children (and adults) can have allergies (indicated by positive skin tests or even hives or hay fever) with or without being asthmatic. It is also possible to be an asthmatic with no allergies, if the asthma is due to a viral illness of the air passages. When an allergen brings on an asthma attack, the culprit is almost always something that has been inhaled, although occasionally foods such as shell fish or peanuts may cause asthma as part of an anaphylactic (massive widespread total body) reaction.

Cat and dog dander, molds, house dust mites, tree grass, and ragweed pollens are common allergens. Cigarette smoke and astringent rubs are irritants *not* allergens, but may nevertheless trigger off an asthma attack just as exercise or cold air can.

FOOD AND DRUG ALLERGY

Although it is rare, food allergy sometimes triggers very severe asthma attacks that can be life-threatening. Nuts and shell fish are common food allergens. *Anaphylaxis,* which consists of a tingling in the mouth and throat, followed by rapid swelling and, sometimes, obstruction of the upper air passages can also cause shock and physical collapse. It is a serious medical emergency that always requires *immediate* attention to prevent death.

Sudden life-threatening asthma can also occur within 30–60 minutes of taking a nonsteroidal anti-inflammatory drug (an NSAID) such as aspirin, ibuprofen, and indomethacin. About one in ten severe asthmatics is sensitive to these NSAIDs.

EXERCISE ASTHMA

Exercise or vigorous activity can trigger asthma, particularly in cold, dry weather. Asthma brought on by exercise indicates poor asthma control. The best treatment is to control exercise asthma with anti-inflammatory medications and use inhaled bronchodilators immediately before exercise. A new long-acting bronchodilator called salmeterol (Serevent) that protects against asthma for 12 hours has been helpful. Asthma should never prevent your children from exercising. Regular exercise may actually improve the asthma. If exercise or play causes problems in spite of vigorous treatment, have your child try swimming since warm, moist air is less likely to trigger asthma.

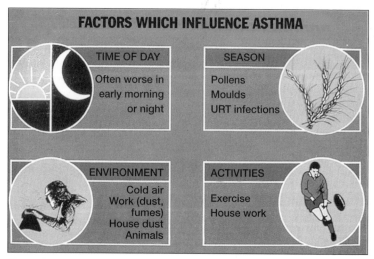

Figure 3–3. Factors that influence asthma.

DAY-CARE AND SCHOOL RELATED ASTHMA

When children start day-care, they are immediately exposed to new viruses, which they pass around. For the first couple of years, viral illnesses can occur as often as every 4–8 weeks after which children build up resistance. In older children, asthma from exposure to triggers at school, such as in a wood shop or from a pet in the classroom, would tend to get worse as the week progresses and improve over the weekend or on vacation. In such situations, however, the child may actually get worse after leaving school because of a *late asthmatic reaction* due to inflammation that reaches a peak 6–8 hours after exposure. This can make it difficult to relate the evening asthma attack to the daytime exposure. Asthma that gets worse on weekends suggests an exposure to allergens or irritants at home.

THE FIRST VISIT TO THE DOCTOR

When you first take your child to the family doctor or specialist, the information you provide (the history) is the single most important piece of the diagnostic "puzzle." Make a list of the symptoms and the circumstances under which they occurred before the visit, provide a clear description of your child's problem, and answer the doctor's questions as precisely as possible.

MILD, MODERATE, AND SEVERE ASTHMA

The *severity* of your child's asthma is related to the type and amount of treatment needed to control the symptoms and restore normal health. Understanding this will help you to take care of your child's asthma.

1. Mild asthma: In mild asthma, the inflammation of the air passages is mild most of the time. Your child's symptoms of cough, breathlessness, and wheezing occur rarely and usually only when triggered by exercise, cold air, or infections. Mild asthmatics almost never need emergency treatment and usually respond extremely well to bronchodilator (reliever) puffers, which are needed fewer than 2–3 times a week or only before exercise. Most of the time, additional medication may not be needed. However, if your child catches a chest cold, a two- to three-week course of inhaled steroids (preventers or controllers) may speed up recovery.

2. Moderate asthma: In moderate asthma, airway inflammation is greater than in mild asthma, symptoms are present almost every day or night, but they rarely interfere with school or play except during bad chest colds. Night wakening is rare, but night time or early morning coughing is common. Children with moderate asthma rarely require treatment in the emergency department or need hospitalization, and with good environmental control measures, regular low-dose medication with anti-inflammatory agents, and occasional use of rescue bronchodilators, they can be kept symptom-free most of the time.

3. Severe asthma: In this severe form, airway inflammation is marked, the airways are always irritable, and symptoms occur daily, and these can be limiting during exertion. Many triggers make the asthma worse, and the child often awakens at night coughing. The chest is often congested in the morning. Children with severe asthma often need to go to the hospital emergency department for treatment, and hospitalization, which may be necessary up to several times a year. In this group of children, severe attacks can occur, and if these are not treated vigorously and early in their course, these attacks can be fatal.

If your child has severe asthma, you must try to keep the problem *under control at all times* and be prepared to increase the doses of medication *early* in the course of flare-ups. Over the long term, relatively high doses of preventive anti-inflammatory medications will usually keep the problem under control.

If they are exposed to large amounts of allergen, or have a viral cold or chest infection, even mild or moderate asthmatics can experience severe attacks that require hospitalization. While freedom from symptoms cannot be guaranteed at all times, the majority of children and adolescents can conquer asthma and lead normal lives free of symptoms, if they minimize exposure to allergens and take their medications regularly and in adequate doses. Once the airway inflammation is firmly under control, and the lungs are again working normally (as shown by normal or best possible tests), which may take several months, the medication can usually be reduced to maintenance doses much lower than those needed to bring the asthma under control.

OUTGROWING ASTHMA

Fifty to 80 percent of children with asthma become symptom free during their teenage years. This is most likely to occur if the asthma has been mild. In about half of such children, the asthma does not come back. Some asthmatics, however, may get worse during their teenage years, and sometimes asthmatic children will improve with the onset of puberty, remain well for 10 or 15 years and then again start to experience asthma in their 30s or 40s (perhaps after a viral infection or a pregnancy).

ALL THAT WHEEZES IS NOT ASTHMA

Wheezing is a nonspecific symptom. It can occur in nonasthmatic conditions such as bronchitis, bronchiolitis, or croup. Four other conditions may mimic asthma, and these are:

1. Inhaled objects: Bits of food, small plastic toys, or anything else that infants or children can get into their mouths can produce asthma-like symptoms. Children should not be given nuts before they are four years old.

2. Stomach acid (gastroesophageal) reflux: Infants often regurgitate, which is why they are burped regularly. When they are awake, infants simply throw up the contents of their stomachs, but if they are asleep, some of this material may get into their lungs and cause irritation and inflammation, which results in asthma-like complaints. In some children stomach acid reflux can lead to pneumonia, and if the problem continues, the lungs may become scarred (fibrosis) or the airway walls badly damaged, leading to frequent or continuous infections (bronchiectasis). The simple clue that this condition is not asthma is that the symptoms fail to fully respond to vigorous asthma treatment. Also, features suggesting other conditions may be present. Investigations to diagnose acid reflux might include esophagus and stomach x-rays, and tests of stomach acid content. Reflux is treated by elevating the bed 4–6 inches (10–15 cm) on blocks. Pillows should not be used to prop the child up because this may make the reflux worse. Children or infants should not be fed within 4 hours of going to bed and should *never* go to bed with a bottle. To these measures may be added medications that speed up the flow of food from the stomach and decrease acidity. In severe cases, surgery may be

needed to tighten the "valve" where the esophagus (gullet) enters the stomach.

3. Chronic bronchitis: Chronic bronchitis is a persistent cough with sputum, which is present on most days of the year. In adults, this is usually caused by smoking. "Chronic bronchitis" in children is usually asthma, but conditions like cystic fibrosis or bronchiectasis due to pneumonia must be excluded as possibilities. Recurring acid aspiration (see above) also causes chronic bronchitis since stomach juices (acid and digestive enzymes) are highly irritating to the lung lining.

4. Psychogenic asthma or vocal cord dysfunction: Children and teenagers under stress may develop wheezing that arises from the voice box (larynx). The wheezing sounds much like asthma. Some of these children may also have asthma as well as the wheezing, which makes the diagnosis difficult. This kind of wheezing is never present at night when the child is sleeping. It tends to worsen when the child is around other people. Occasionally, this is an attention-getting mechanism and may follow a respiratory infection during which the child enjoyed a lot of attention because of the wheezing. For reasons that are unclear, "psychogenic asthma" is seen more in adolescent girls. To complicate things further, almost any type of inhaler therapy can produce temporary relief. Diagnostic clues include (1) very loud wheezing, (2) a child who looks distressed, but is not breathless, and (3) the noise mostly coming from the throat rather than the lungs. Making the diagnosis requires considering the possibility of psychogenic asthma and then measuring lung function; this is often normal during an "attack" or is not reproducible. Also when viewed with the bronchoscope, the vocal cords stay closed, which is in contrast to a normal situation, where they open on breathing in.

Treatment of this stress-related (or psychogenic) problem requires proper testing to exclude asthma, withdrawal of unnecessary medication (often including asthma puffers), a sympathetic doctor, and parents and child willing to consider the diagnosis. The family must also be prepared to recognize and deal with the stresses that brought on the condition.

TABLE 3–1 Are Your Child's Symptoms Due to Asthma?*		
Check List	Yes	No
Coughing and wheezing at night that keeps recurring	–	–
Tightness in the chest, wheezing, or breathlessness in cold weather, particularly with exercise	–	–
A cough that does not get better within 4 weeks following a viral cold	–	–
Greater than usual breathlessness after exercise	–	–
Tight chest and shortness of breath after eating certain foods	–	–
Allergic symptoms like eczema, itchy eyes, or itchy runny nose and cough	–	–

*If *any* of the above is "yes," your child may have asthma, and if *several* are "yes," a diagnosis of asthma is highly likely.

CHAPTER FOUR

ASTHMA TRIGGERS

Many different things can set off an asthma attack, and different situations act as triggers in different people. However, if the asthma *is under control*, as a rule, triggers cause little or no difficulty.

ALLERGIC FACTORS

The most common trigger of asthma is allergy, but viral infections are a more common trigger than allergies in infants and toddlers up to about age 6. Inhaling an allergic substance (allergen) such as grass pollen, house dust mites or mold spores can cause wheezing to begin within a few minutes, with recovery 1 or 2 hours later. Another, more persistent attack may follow about 6 hours later. The next day, the airways are even more "twitchy," and after a single exposure, the inflammation and the resulting increased sensitivity of the air passages may go on for 2 or 3 weeks. Ongoing injury to the lining of the airways during continued exposure may produce long-lasting inflammation. If left untreated, after a period of months or years, permanent injury to the airways can occur.

Figure 4–1. House dust mite.

In the spring (trees), summer (grass), and fall (ragweed), when pollen grains are breathed in over several weeks, the airways become inflamed and irritable. This leads to persisting symptoms. Exposure to pollens can be decreased with air conditioning but cannot be completely eliminated. On the other hand, if house dust is the problem, good dust control measures can be very effective.

For some children, family pets are a major trigger, but even when the problem is serious, some families are loathe to get rid of them. It goes a long way to minimize exposure if the pet is kept completely away from the child and out of the family living and sleeping quarters. Regular washing of the pet may also help.

Figure 4–2. Pets can be a major asthma trigger.

EXERCISING, LAUGHING, AND CRYING

Cough or wheezing with chest tightness and breathlessness that comes on after exercise, laughter, or crying is common in asthma. Continuing the exercise may cause gradual improvement. Some asthmatics notice that they can "run through" the asthma or do better if they "warm up" before exercising.

Why Do Asthmatics Get Wheezy On Exercising?
With exercise, breathing becomes faster and deeper. This causes cooling and drying of the airway lining. Asthma can also be triggered if you simply breathe too quickly (hyperventilate). Cold air makes this worse because it draws even more

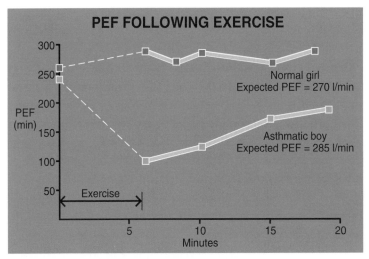

Figure 4–3. Considerable airway narrowing (PEF change) occurred after about 5 or 6 minutes of running, in a boy with asthma. Similar exercise had no effect on a normal girl.

moisture from the lining of the airway. Swimming, however, is thought to decrease the tendency to develop asthma. Exercise-related asthma can usually be confirmed by bicycle or treadmill exercise in the pulmonary function laboratory.

WEATHER, TEMPERATURE, AND HUMIDITY

A sudden change in the air temperature can trigger wheezing. Some children with asthma have difficulty with humid conditions, and this may be, in part, because of an increase in allergens, particularly mold spores, that are released after rainstorms. On the other hand, after a dry spell, grass pollen levels can be higher. Even taking a shower can sometimes trigger an asthma attack. This is because the water aerosol irritates the "twitchy" asthmatic airways.

AIR POLLUTION

In highly industrialized cities, thermal inversions that occur particularly during the spring and fall can result in high levels of air pollution. This can cause worsening of asthma, particularly if it is not under control. Research has shown that during thermal inversions many more asthmatics visit emergency departments.

WHEEZING AT NIGHT

Persons with poorly controlled asthma often wake up in the early morning hours regardless of when they went to sleep. Viral colds may also trigger night time flare-ups, even when the asthma has previously been well controlled. Asthma attacks disturb sleep during the night and interfere with day-time activities.

Wheezing at night is *always* a sign of asthma that is *out of control*, and indicates the need to increase preventive anti-inflammatory medications. This is true, even though at the time of the episode, rapid relief can be obtained by using bronchodilator relievers. Why the problem is generally more severe at night is not certain, but it may be related to a decrease in levels of adrenalin and cortisone that occurs during the night and an accompanying increase in the activity of the bronchoconstrictor nerves. Night-time asthma can almost always be controlled with the use of regular inhaled anti-inflammatory medications; however, the addition of long-acting beta-agonist bronchodilators (like salmeterol) may be helpful if, despite the regular use of high-dose inhaled steroids, asthma remains poorly controlled. Whenever night-time asthma is a problem, it is also important to allergy-proof the bedroom.

INFECTIONS

Asthma often worsens during viral chest infections, which may cause severe and sometimes life-threatening attacks. The influenza virus can damage the lining of the airways and cause increased inflammation which, if not brought under control with anti-inflammatory treatment, can last for many weeks. Sinus infections can also make asthma worse if they are not treated with antibiotics. Most children with asthma should receive an influenza immunization each fall.

STRESS AND EMOTIONAL FACTORS

Stress, anxiety, or anger do not *cause* asthma, but they can be trigger factors in some patients, if their asthma has not been kept under firm control. The mechanism that causes the onset of asthma in these circumstances is thought to be hyperventilation and subsequent cooling of the airways as occurs during exercise.

MEDICATIONS AS TRIGGERS

Nonsteroidal anti-inflammatory drugs (NSAIDs e.g., aspirin) may trigger a severe asthma attack within 15–40 minutes of taking them. NSAID-related asthma usually occurs in older asthmatics who are not allergic to the more usual pollens, domestic animals, and house dust. These patients often have sinus problems and polyps in the nose. Even a single aspirin tablet can trigger a severe attack, which usually starts with a runny nose and a flushed face.

CHAPTER FIVE

HOW DOCTORS TEST FOR ASTHMA

BREATHING TESTS

Pulmonary Function Tests

Breathing tests can help establish a diagnosis of asthma as well as measure its severity. The amount of air that can be rapidly forced out of the child's lungs each second (the one-second forced expired volume or FEV_1) is reduced in proportion to the narrowing of the air passages. The laboratory instrument most commonly used to measure how well your child's lungs are working is called a spirometer. When your child breathes in as deeply as possible and then exhales rapidly into the mouthpiece, a computer measures how much air is blown out within one-second. The narrower the air passages, the smaller the FEV_1. The total amount of air breathed out until the lungs are empty is also measured (the forced vital capacity or FVC); this can also be reduced in asthma because of trapped air. When this test is repeated after administering a bronchodilator to open up the airways, a considerable improvement usually occurs in children with asthma. This simple and painless test can be done in most children over the age of 5. In specialized centers, a similar test can be done in sedated infants less than 2 years of age.

PEAK FLOW METERS AND CHARTS

An even simpler breathing test, which can be done at home with an inexpensive device, is peak flow measurement. A peak flow meter reliably measures airway narrowing, and can easily be carried around. The measurement takes only a minute. This test is even better for diagnosing asthma than a single spirometer test done in a clinic, because asthma is variable and a test may be normal when the measurement is made in the doctor's office. Since asthma symptoms are generally worse at night or first thing in the morning, having a peak flow meter at home allows you to measure the severity at the time the symptoms are present. Also, the response to treatment can be measured and so provide a long-term perspective of the problem for you and your doctor. The peak flow meter measures the maximum speed with which air can be blown out of the lungs after a full breath has been taken in. The test is usually repeated three times, and the best result can be read directly from the scale on the instrument. Usually you will be asked to measure the peak flow in the morning and at night and record it on a chart. The chart can be used to record medications and symptoms and allows you to see how your child responds to various treatments. The chart that we have developed for use at the Brenner Children's Hospital and Wake Forest University School of Medicine in Winston-Salem, North Carolina, is reproduced on page 33. Make as many copies of this chart as you need.

EXERCISE TESTS

An exercise test in a laboratory may be helpful in children who only get asthma with exercise, but otherwise have normal lung function tests. This test is performed by having the child exercise as much as possible, while measuring breathing and heart rate. Lung function testing is repeated after exercise to see if it has decreased during the test. Exercise testing can help your doctor tell the difference between breathing problems, heart problems, or poor muscle conditioning as the cause of breathlessness with exercise.

ALLERGY SKIN TESTS

To confirm that allergy is present, skin testing may be recommended for your child. The tests consist of skin scratch tests; allergens from different classes (molds, pollens, household pets, house dust mites, and sometimes food in very young children) are used. A drop of allergen is placed on the skin, which is then pricked with a small needle. Positive reactions produce itching after 5 minutes, formation of a small blister (wheal) and reddening of the surrounding area (flare), which last an hour or two. Some reactions may be greater than others, but this does not necessarily relate to the severity of the allergy. About 20% of people without symptoms of allergy can have positive skin tests. The things that you have observed to produce asthma symptoms in your child (e.g., cats) are most important in establishing the cause of asthma, and skin tests can confirm this. Skin tests may also lead to consideration of factors not previously thought of. Some people with asthma do not have skin reactions, since asthma is also triggered by some nonallergic factors.

CHEST X–RAY

In asthma, unless the problem is severe or complicated, a chest x-ray is rarely needed. Shadows may show up on x-ray, however, because of plugs of mucus blocking the air passages. During an attack, the lungs are usually overinflated

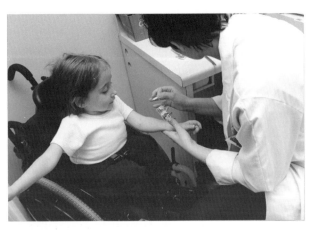

Figure 5–1.   Allergy skin testing.

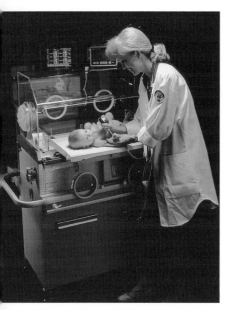

Figure 5–2. Infant pulmonary function testing (with permission from SensorMedics Corporation).

with trapped air. A mold called *Aspergillus* can also cause severe asthma and permanent inflammatory changes in the airways. In this situation, damaged distended airways, full of secretions may show up on the x-ray and assist with the diagnosis. Occasionally, the overinflation of the lungs becomes so severe that air may pass through ruptured air sacs and spread into the pleural space around the lungs. This may cause one, or very rarely both, lungs to collapse (p n e u m o t h o r a x). Pneumothorax can sometimes lead to large amounts of air collecting in the pleural space and build up such high levels of air pressure that the heart can no longer pump the blood effectively. Death can result unless the problem is quickly treated by inserting a needle into the chest to let the air escape.

CHALLENGE TESTS

Asthma challenge tests can be useful when asthma is suspected, but other tests are normal. Challenge tests measure the degree of "twitchiness" of the airways by using a fine mist of a medication that causes transient airway narrowing. Usually, histamine or methacholine are used. The test measures the "amount" of the provoking substance required to narrow the airways as measured by a spirometer. The greater the twitchiness, the smaller the amount of provoking substance needed, and this indicates that the asthma is more severe and that more anti-inflammatory medication will be needed to achieve control. On rare occasions, patients with asthma are given an aerosol of an allergic substance or chemical to which they may be sensitive, to see if this will provoke a mild asthma attack. This is occasionally useful for finding the cause of asthma, but the test is considered experimental. Since this test may precipitate severe asthma, it should only be done under careful supervision by doctor in a suitable laboratory.

HOME MONITORING

Like regular measurement of blood pressure in patients with high blood pressure, the best way to be sure that an asthma treatment is working well (apart from freedom from symptoms) is to measure peak flow regularly. Peak flow can act as an early warning of deterioration and allow you or your child to make adjustments in medication before the situation becomes serious. Peak flow readings help to establish the *pattern* of asthma, and this can assist you and your doctor to select the correct form of treatment and dose. Peak flow may reveal that the asthma is more, or less, severe than you or your doctor think. During flare-ups, if you phone for assistance, provision of peak flow measurements will help your doctor to determine the severity of the problem and decide on the best treatment.

The newer peak flow meters are divided into "zones." Ideally the peak flow reading stays in the "green" zone, which indicates at least 80% of the predicted or best achievable value. If the result is nearly always in this range, your child's asthma is under control, and after several months, your doctor may wish to start decreasing the medication to the "minimum maintenance dose." In the yellow (caution) zone, peak flow readings are 50–80% of your child's predicted, or best, possible result.

Asthma Centre for Children
Brenner Children's Hospital
Medical Center Blvd.
Winston-Salem, NC 27157-1081
Telephone 800-277-7654

ASTHMA DAILY
RECORD CARD

Date this card was started:

			1	2	3	4	5

1. WHEEZE LAST NIGHT	Good Night 0	Woke through the night because of wheeze 2
	Slept well but slightly wheezy . . .1	
2. COUGH LAST NIGHT	None 0	Severe 2
	Some, but slept through it 1	
3. WHEEZE TODAY	None 0	Severe 2
	Little 1	
4. ACTIVITY TODAY	Normal 0	Much reduced activity: Had to stay home 2
	Some shortness of breath 1	

5. LIST ALL MEDICINES AND DOSES.

Peak Flow Zones

ME ME ME ME ME

500—
400—
300—
200—
100—
000—

6. COMMENTS   Note if you had exposure to a known trigger (1) or last visit to the doctor or emergency room (E).

Figure 5–3. The peak-flow diary card for children.

The yellow zone is an early warning that suggests the need for additional medication to prevent further deterioration. The earliest sign of poor asthma control may be a "green zone" reading in the evening, but a "yellow zone" in the early morning, with the peak flow rising into the green zone after inhaling a bronchodilator. This so-called "morning dipping" may mean that additional attention may need to be given to the bedroom environment (e.g., house dust mite control measures) or that the annual tree pollen season is just starting. If this occurs two days in a row, you should increase the preventer medication, usually to twice the maintenance dose, to improve control of the airway inflammation. The larger dose should be continued for 1 to 2 weeks.

Persistent readings in the yellow zone, or a reading that dips into the red or danger zone — less than 50% of predicted best — may warn of an impending severe asthma attack that demands immediate action. You should call your child's doctor, and you may need to start oral steroid medication (e.g., prednisone) to bring the asthma under rapid control. Children with well-controlled asthma, who regularly take their prescribed doses of medication and use their inhalers effectively, rarely get red zone readings, except perhaps during viral chest infections when vigorous additional treatment is often required. Once the asthma is under control, and you are confident of dealing with it relatively effectively, it may not be necessary to measure peak flow as frequently. You should continue to check it once or twice a week, and if your child becomes breathless, you should revert to measuring it regularly twice a day (or sometimes even more frequently), before and after the reliever (bronchodilator) medication. If your child has attacks from time to time, it is a good idea to try to record the peak flow at the time to determine the severity and how much improvement treatment brings about. You should notify your child's doctor about these episodes, and *please* always take the peak flow charts, meter, and all medications to the follow-up visits with your doctor.

SPUTUM EVALUATION

This test can help your doctor determine if the cause of the cough is asthma rather than chest infection. Eosinophils are almost always present (so called eosinophilic bronchitis) as a "marker" of asthma. It is quite easy to count the proportion of eosinophils in phlegm routinely to help confirm that asthma is present or less than optimally treated. It also confirms if a flare-up is due to asthma (mainly eosinophils) or to infection (mainly neutrophils). This test is very useful because asthma is best treated with steroids while infection may require antibiotics.

HOW ASTHMA TREATMENTS WORK

PREVENTION

The basic principles of treating childhood asthma are the same as those for treating adults. The most important step is to eliminate or avoid identified (or suspected) allergens, such as household pets or house dust mites, pollens or molds, and irritants like tobacco and wood burning stoves.

INFLUENZA VACCINATION

The "flu" vaccine is useful for protection against the more severe "influenza" viruses, and it should be given annually in the fall or early winter. Flu vaccine is not recommended for children less than 3 months of age. Children less than 1 year often have their shot split into two doses given 4 weeks apart. Children who are allergic to eggs should not receive the flu vaccine unless they have been evaluated by an allergist. This is because the vaccine is grown in an egg medium.

MEDICATIONS

Two main classes (types) of medication are used to treat asthma: bronchodilators or relievers, and anti-inflammatory medications or preventers.

Bronchodilators (Relievers)

The choice of bronchodilators for children is the same as for adults: beta-agonist inhalers are usually best, but in some asthmatics, anticholinergic bronchodilators like Atrovent may be useful, especially for those asthmatics who experience excessive shakiness, tremor, and rapid heart beat when on beta agonists. The combination of Atrovent and beta agonists is sometimes more effective than beta agonists alone.

Anti-inflammatory Medications (Preventers)

Cromolyn (Intal) is used in mild-to-moderate asthma, but is not very effective in severe asthma. The usual dose is 2-5 puffs, four times per day. The strength of the dose per puff is five times greater in Europe and the UK than it is in the USA and Canada. Very small doses of inhaled steroids are equivalent to maximum useful doses of cromolyn, and since such treatment is easier, less expensive, and does not have significant side effects, many physicians prefer inhaled steroids to cromolyn, even in relatively mild asthma. Nedocromil (Tilade) is a newer form of anti-inflammatory inhaler that is similar to cromolyn, but that is slightly more effective. Many patients experience a bad taste when taking nedocromil. This can be relieved by using an aerosol holding chamber that screens out the larger particles that impact the taste buds in the mouth. If nedocromil is effective, it is more convenient than Intal because it can be given two or three times a day and thus need not be taken to school. Inhaled steroids are effective in children and are relatively inexpensive. Below 500 micrograms (mcg) per day, few side effects have been reported, even in very young children. If steroid inhalers are used with a holding chamber, which reduces the total body dose, up to 800–1,000 mcg/day can be used over long periods of time, with few or no side effects. It has been suggested that inhaled steroids might decrease growth rate, but this is hard to determine since children also tend to have decreased growth rate if their asthma is out of control. If moderate doses are used, effective treatment is more likely to restore the growth rate to normal. Inhaled steroids usually work well when given twice a day, making it easier for parents to supervise their child's care. Add-on devices for steroid inhalers include the AeroChamber (the AeroChamber comes with a mouthpiece for children over age 4 and a mask for neonates, toddlers, and children up to age 2–3 years), the Volumatic, Inspirease, and a number of other add-ons. These devices should always be used in children who need inhaled steroids to achieve asthma control because they decrease steroid side effects. This decrease is accomplished by reducing the local dose to the throat and larynx by 90% and the total body dose to only 25% of what it would be without the metered dose inhaler (MDI) add-on device.

Oral steroids, in pill or syrup form, are only used over periods of weeks or months to treat children with the most severe asthma that does not respond to inhaled medications. Fortunately, this is rarely necessary. The lowest dose required to control symptoms should be given, if possible, on alternate days together with the other medications outlined above. Any child taking a high-dose inhaled steroid (over 800 mcg/d of beclomethasone), or who needs oral steroids more than once per year, should be periodically evaluated or cared for by a specialist. Asthma control, growth, and possible side effects should be carefully monitored.

OTHER MEDICATIONS

Steroid Sparing Agents
If a child's asthma is very severe and requires large daily doses of oral steroids, very powerful medications such as methotrexate or cyclosporin, which reduce the activity of the immune system, are sometimes tried. These medications can have serious side effects, but research is ongoing to develop an aerosol inhalation delivery with fewer side effects. Oral steroids (in the lowest possible maintenance dose) must only be used under the care of an asthma specialist and only after repeated attempts to reduce the steroid tablet dose when inhaled steroids have failed.

Antihistamines
Histamine is a chemical released from white blood cells. Patients with asthma release histamine in excessive amounts. Histamine can trigger an allergic reaction accompanied by

wheezing, red itchy eyes, and a runny nose — symptoms typical of hay fever. Antihistamines block many of the nasal symptoms, but are much less effective in treating asthma. If used with steroids and epinephrine, antihistamines can be useful during a widespread reaction accompanied by hives.

Cough Medications and Decongestants

The nasal congestion that is common in children with asthma often forces them to breathe through their mouth. This often becomes worse at night and may be associated with snoring. Cough may be due to asthma or to a postnasal mucus drip. This problem is best dealt with by controlling the inflammation that causes the asthma and rhinitis. In asthma, there is little role for cough suppressant medications or decongestants as these do not treat the underlying inflammation. These medications may, however, be useful if a cough is not due to asthma.

INHALERS, TABLETS, OR LIQUIDS?

Research has shown that inhalers are much more effective than oral medications for treating asthma. Metered dose inhalers (MDIs), or puffers as they are sometimes called, may be difficult for children under age 5 to use. They will have less difficulty, however, if aerosol holding chambers containing a valve are used with the MDI. Children can then breathe in and out normally from the device with a mouthpiece, if they are older, or from a mask, if they are under about 4 years of age. This ensures that they actually get the medication. Powder inhalers may not work in children under 6, particularly during severe attacks. This is because of the effort needed to release the powder. Nebulizers, which are used with liquid solutions, were generally used in infants and young children in the past, but these are rapidly being replaced in hospitals and homes by MDIs fitted with valved holding chambers. These not only ensure aerosol delivery to infants and young children, but they are also easier to use, more effective, reduce side effects, and cost much less. At times, many MDI puffs of bronchodilator medication (e.g., Proventil or Ventolin) may be needed to rescue the child from a severe attack. Sometimes up to 12 puffs are given over a period of 10 minutes (a total of about 1 mg) to provide the equivalent of a nebulizer treatment (5 mg in the nebulizer). In the past, it was not fully understood that the difference in benefit was not related to the device, but rather to the very much larger dose commonly given by the nebulizer compared to the usual 2 or 3 puffs delivered by an MDI. If a child really does need a nebulizer because multiple MDI puffs do not seem to reverse the attack (rarely), it should always be used under the care of a specialist.

Because children may be embarrassed to use an inhaler at school, twice daily inhaled steroids are convenient. Occasionally, in more severe asthma, even when the same total dose is used, administration of the steroid medication 3 or 4 times a day works better. Children able to handle their inhaler reliably (over about age 5 or 6) should carry their bronchodilator MDI for *self-care* of asthma attacks. To enable them to do this, they may need a note to the school principal or nurse. See an example of such a letter on page 86. If your child is in day-care or in kindergarten, the parents should instruct their care-givers in the use of their child's medications. Following severe asthma attacks, additional treatment with oral steroids (prednisone, usually) may be needed for 3–10 days or longer. Contact your doctor as soon as possible if the asthma attack recurs or persists. If your child is very breathless, take him or her to the closest health care facility at once. An asthma attack means that your child's asthma is out of control. This situation must be treated at once to prevent serious illness or even death.

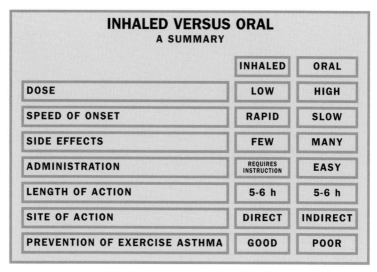

INHALED VERSUS ORAL
A SUMMARY

	INHALED	ORAL
DOSE	LOW	HIGH
SPEED OF ONSET	RAPID	SLOW
SIDE EFFECTS	FEW	MANY
ADMINISTRATION	REQUIRES INSTRUCTION	EASY
LENGTH OF ACTION	5-6 h	5-6 h
SITE OF ACTION	DIRECT	INDIRECT
PREVENTION OF EXERCISE ASTHMA	GOOD	POOR

Figure 6–1. A comparison of oral and inhaled medications.

Taking Medicines by Mouth Versus by Inhalation

Children sometimes dislike taking tablets or syrups and aerosols are much more effective and cause fewer side effects. Whenever possible liquids or tablets should be replaced by aerosol treatment with anti-inflammatory (preventer) and bronchodilator (reliever) puffers.

BRONCHODILATORS: ASTHMA RELIEVERS

There are three types of bronchodilator drug and these are sympathomimetics (epinephrine), theophylline (caffeine), and anticholinergics (belladonna or atropine).

Sympathomimetics
(Albuterol/Salbutamol-Like Medications)

Sympathomimetic bronchodilators (relievers) come from adrenalin, the "fight or flight" hormone, which is released from two small glands above the kidneys (adrenal glands). Adrenalin or epinephrine is the biochemical signal of the sympathetic nervous system that responds to stress. Drugs that act in the same way are called sympathomimetics (i.e., they mimic the action of adrenalin).

Epinephrine (Adrenalin) and Its Synthetic Derivatives

Epinephrine was used to treat asthma almost 100 years ago. It was and still is very effective for rapid relief of symptoms and can be given by injection or inhalation. In some countries, it is still used for treatment of severe attacks. Because it could not be given by mouth, lasted for only 30–60 minutes, and caused heart palpitations and shakiness in most people, it was replaced by more "selective" sympathomimetics that provided the same benefits but had far fewer side effects and a longer duration of action. Adrenalin is still one of the best rescue treatments for anaphylaxis.

Beta$_2$ Sympathomimetics: Longer Action and Fewer Side Effects

The beta$_2$ sympathomimetics are longer acting epinephrine-like drugs that work for 4–6 hours, can readily be inhaled, and have few side effects. The best known of these is salbutamol (called albuterol in the USA). It is sold under the trade names Ventolin, and Proventil. Terbutaline (Bricanyl), procaterol (Proair), and pirbuterol (Maxair) are other beta$_2$ agonists. Recently new bronchodilators that work for about 12 hours have been developed including salmeterol (Serevent) and formoterol (Foradil).

How Do They Work?   Beta agonists relax airway smooth muscles to relieve episodes of wheezing. Most beta agonists last for less than their usual time when the asthma is out of control, which is a good indication of the severity of the flare-up. Most infants and children are able to inhale beta agonists from a puffer and holding chamber, although some may occasionally need to use a nebulizer. If taken before exercise or exposure to cold air, these drugs can also be used to prevent wheezing. Protection lasts up to 2 hours with the shorter-acting drugs like albuterol/salbutamol and for 8–12 hours with salmeterol and formoterol. It should be emphasized that the shorter-acting beta agonists relieve symptoms within a few minutes, but that salmeterol does not act as quickly. It takes at least 30 minutes to *begin* working and so should *not* be used for sudden asthma attacks. Formoterol, on the other hand, has a rapid onset of action like that of salbutamol and, therefore, can be used for rapid relief of an asthma attack. These bronchodilators may provide partial relief of symptoms, but they do not "cool down" the inflammation in the airways, and parents may be deceived into thinking that their child's asthma is better when the inflammation is merely masked. If your child needs beta agonists even three times a week regularly (unless exercise is the only trigger), then an anti-inflammatory treatment should be added and *taken every day*. Treating asthma with bronchodilators alone is like treating appendicitis with just pain relievers rather than by removing the inflamed appendix!

Side Effects When given by an inhaler, the beta-agonist medications have few side effects. They are *safe* to use up to 6 to 8 times in a 24-hour day although *this indicates that the asthma is not under control*. They are also safe to use in an acute severe asthma attack in a dose of up to 10 or 15 puffs, over a period of about 10 minutes, repeated, if necessary every 30 minutes while the attack is severe. These medications do not lose their effect over time, and there is no danger of addiction. The most common side effect is shakiness and, sometimes, rapid heartbeat. The side effects tend to decrease the more the drug is used, even though the beneficial effects do not decrease. Recent studies have suggested that *more than necessary* long-term overuse of beta agonists might even make asthma worse.

Theophylline

Theophylline is a bronchodilator medication available only in oral form (as liquid, tablets or sprinkles). It has a very small effect on inflammation. Theophylline is not as potent as the beta agonists as an asthma reliever, and when combined with them, adds no additional benefit for most people. Today, with good anti-inflammatory treatment and long-acting beta-agonist inhalers, theophylline is being used much less. Depending upon the dose taken and absorbed, theophylline can sometimes cause side effects. These side effects are similar to those you get from drinking too much coffee and, indeed, theophylline and caffeine are closely related drugs. These side effects can include nausea, indigestion, a feeling of anxiety, headache, inability to sleep, and shakiness. The dose level of theophylline in the blood must be monitored carefully to avoid overdosing, which can cause serious side effects such as seizures and even death. In some children, theophylline is thought to cause poor concentration in school and hyperactivity. Some people are more susceptible to these side effects and others have little difficulty. To be sure that this drug is in the safe range and not dangerously high or uselessly low, blood levels are usually measured, more often when the medication is first started. Even so, the blood level can change because of a number of factors, including age, viral illness, smoking, certain foods, and many medications. Also, different people absorb the same dose of theophylline differently. Not surprisingly, most doctors rarely use theophylline unless absolutely necessary.

Anticholinergics

These bronchodilators block the cholinergic nerves, which contribute to narrowing of the air passages because they stimulate the airway muscle to contract. The only medication of this class used widely is ipratropium bromide (Atrovent), which is available by inhaler or nebulizer. It lasts up to

8 hours, may be useful in a serious asthma attack along with beta agonists, but is not as effective as the latter when the asthma is stable. Atrovent has few side effects, except for a dry mouth.

WHICH BRONCHODILATOR IS BEST?

The most effective and versatile bronchodilator drugs, and the ones with the fewest side effects, are the inhaled beta agonists. Many of these are available, and most of them act in a very similar fashion for about 3 to 6 hours. The newer beta agonists (salmeterol, formoterol) can last for 12 hours or more. Theophylline is a weaker bronchodilator and may cause troublesome side effects. Anticholinergics are the weakest bronchodilators for asthma but are effective in chronic bronchitis and cystic fibrosis. In an acute asthma attack, combining anticholinergics and beta agonists may provide better relief than beta agonists used alone.

Unfortunately, none of these medications decreases the underlying airway inflammation that actually leads to asthma. *These medications should never be used by themselves for control of asthma unless it is very mild and the need for bronchodilators is rare* (e.g., not more than 1 to 2 times a week or only before exercise).

ANTI-INFLAMMATORY DRUGS: ASTHMA PREVENTERS AND CONTROLLERS

Relieving inflammation in asthma usually leads to prevention of symptoms and greatly reduces the need for bronchodilator drugs. Three main treatments are available: corticosteroids, cromolyn, and nedocromil. A new class of asthma medicines that block part of the inflammatory chain of events (the leukotriene D_4 blockers) have recently become available, but are not yet approved for use in children.

Corticosteroids (Steroids)

Corticosteroids are a class of hormones produced naturally in the body, and they are the most effective anti-asthma treatment presently available. They are sometimes *underused*. This is because many patients (and some doctors) are afraid of steroids. You may have read about testosterone-like steroid abuse by Olympic athletes who used them to build muscles. This is a very different steroid from the type used to treat asthma and other inflammatory diseases. The steroids used to control asthma are almost always given by inhalation in small doses, so that the side effects commonly associated with long-term use of oral steroids (including tablets and syrups) or injections are virtually nonexistent. Furthermore, even oral steroids used for short periods of time to control a severe attack of asthma rarely cause side effects of concern, that is, unless they are used for *more than 3 or 4 weeks or repeatedly for 1 or 2 weeks with only 1 or 2 weeks between courses of treatment*. In children with severe asthma flare-ups, 5 to 14 days of steroids by mouth usually control the attack. Such treatment is very safe and effective.

How Do Steroids Work?   Steroids suppress inflammation. This is why they are very effective in controlling asthma. Unlike bronchodilator relievers that act within minutes, steroids take a few hours to begin to act, but the effect is longer lasting. Steroids control the *cause* of asthma rather than the resulting muscle spasm that is reversed by bronchodilator medications.

Steroid Inhalers   Steroid inhalers have been available for over 25 years. They are probably the single greatest advance in asthma treatment. Small doses of the steroid are inhaled and deposited on the surface of the airway, where they suppress inflammation. Very little steroid is absorbed into the blood and even that is rapidly inactivated in the liver so that side effects are almost nonexistent, except when extremely large doses (over 500–800 mcg/d) are needed. Side effects are still *much less* than would be seen if a similarly effective daily dose is given orally (10–20 mg). Steroid inhalers include beclomethasone (Becotide, Beclovent, Vanceril, Becloforte), fluticasone (Flovent), and budesonide (Pulmicort). Other inhaled steroids available in the USA and Canada include flunisolide (Bronalide, AeroBid), and triamcinolone acetonide (Azmacort). Steroid inhalers must be taken *regularly* to control asthma. They take effect within a few days, but up to 8 to 10 weeks may pass before the effect is at its maximum. This is because long-standing inflammation causes plugging of smaller airways that can take a long time to clear. Inhaled steroids act for up to 12 hours and can usually be taken twice daily. The inhaler left by your child's toothbrush can act as a reminder to use both twice daily. These medications are preventers, and you should not expect to see the immediate relief of an asthma attack that only bronchodilators can provide. Some patients misunderstand how inhaled steroids work and feel that the relievers are not as "good" as the bronchodilator puffers. In some chronic asthmatics, *the regular use of inhaled steroids* may be necessary *lifelong*. With good control of the asthma, bronchodilators will probably be required only occasionally unless the asthma becomes severe, such as when your child is exposed to allergens or develops a viral "flu."

Side Effects   Side effects of inhaled steroids are uncommon especially if a holding chamber (see Chapter 9) is used with the puffer. A sore mouth and throat may develop due to yeast infection (thrush), which is recognized by white spots inside the mouth. Yeast infections are more common when high doses of inhaled steroids are used without a holding chamber. People with immune problems or those taking antibiotics are also more susceptible to thrush, which can be treated with 7 to 10 days of medicated lozenges or liquids (Nystatin) or a single dose of antifungal tablets (e.g., fluconazole). About half the patients on high-dose inhaled steroids experience some change in their voice. This complication occurs only rarely when a holding chamber is used with the MDI puffer because it filters out large medication particles and reduces the amount of steroid that deposits in the mouth by 90% without reducing the amount that gets into the lungs. Very uncommon side effects can occur when more than 2000 mcg/day of beclomethasone (or equivalent) is being taken and can include easy bruising and thinning of the skin in adults and possibly a slightly slowed growth *rate* in children. To put this into context, remember that poorly controlled asthma also reduces growth rate in children. At high doses of inhaled steroids, the adrenal glands may respond less well to stress and small cataracts may develop. These usually disappear when the steroid dose is reduced.

Some people complain that some steroid inhalers taste bad (which is subjective). If your child experiences bad taste, he or she could be switched to a different inhaler with similar benefits. An aerosol holding chamber will usually eliminate most of the unpleasant taste of these inhalers.

Systemic Steroids

Asthma control can, at times, deteriorate in spite of adequate doses of inhaled steroids. In such cases, it may become necessary to take the steroids by mouth. Although steroids are very effective taken in this way, they can cause side effects with long term use (generally after 8 weeks or longer), so the *lowest* effective dose should always be used. For the greatest effect, it is best to take this medication in the early afternoon with food, if this is convenient. The most commonly used steroids are prednisone and methylprednisolone. These are very similar and given in the same doses.

In *very* severe asthma oral steroids may be needed every day or, preferably, on alternate days. Oral steroids are taken along with inhaled steroid medications used in maximum doses. If asthma has been controlled for long periods of time by the inhaled anti–inflammatory puffer, it can deteriorate during an infection or after a large exposure to allergen. It is usually then that steroids by mouth may need to be given for a time. For smaller children, the dose is usually 0.5 mg to 1 mg for each pound of body weight taken for 7 to 14 days. The dose is then reduced to the lowest possible needed to maintain asthma control, or discontinued, with inhaled steroids used as maintenance therapy. A rule of thumb is that oral steroids should be continued until your child's symptoms and peak flow reading return to normal or the previous "best" value.

If high doses of oral steroids are needed for many months or years, there may be acne, weight gain, excess hair, thinning of bones, and high blood pressure in children. Oral steroids can cause stunted growth (this does not occur with inhaled steroids in the usual doses). High doses may expose a previous tendency to diabetes. Rarely, the hip joint may be destroyed by loss of blood supply (avascular necrosis).

If long-term oral steroids are stopped abruptly, a state of shock can develop accompanied by low blood pressure, vomiting, and sweatiness. If your child has been on prednisone for a long time and is switched to inhaled steroids for asthma control, the oral steroid should be tapered very slowly to ensure that the adrenal glands have recovered before the prednisone is reduced below about 10 mg per day.

For really good control of asthma, occasionally a small additional dose of prednisone may need to be added to the inhaled steroids. This dose may make all the difference in stabilizing what is otherwise difficult asthma.

CROMOLYN (INTAL) AND NEDOCROMIL (TILADE)

Nedocromil, a more recent medication than cromolyn, has anti-allergic properties. Both cromolyn and nedocromil are inhaled from MDIs or given by a nebulizer. Neither medication is a bronchodilator, but both can prevent asthma episodes if taken 15 to 30 minutes before exposure to known allergens or before exercise or cold air exposure. It is not known exactly how they work, but they do seem to decrease the release of constrictor chemicals from mast cells. They are taken 3 to 4 times daily, and it may take weeks before improvement is noted. They are less effective than steroids and are only sometimes helpful when added to inhaled steroids.

KETOTIFEN (ZADITEN)

This is a type of antihistamine that may benefit some children with mild asthma. It is taken by mouth, takes several weeks or months to show any benefit, and may be associated with drowsiness and weight gain. It is much less effective and more expensive than inhaled steroids or cromolyn. It is not useful to combine it with the latter, and there is little to recommend the use of this medication in most asthmatics. Ketotifen is not available in the USA.

LEUKOTRIENE–D$_4$ ANTAGONISTS (LTD$_4$)

This is a new class of asthma medicines. These medications are available in tablets, but are not yet approved for use in children. The first of these is Accolate (zafirleukast). Others will soon be available. They are not bronchodilators; they are preventers with a narrow range of action. These medications act by blocking the effect of one of the most powerful inflammation-causing chemicals produced in the body.

Research studies have shown Accolate to be particularly useful in blocking aspirin-induced asthma. It also partly blocks the triggering effect of cold air, exercise, methacholine, and allergens which suggest that this group of medicines may be used alone in mild and exercise-triggered asthma or to help stabilize control in some asthmatic children. At the time of writing, there has been too little experience with these medicines to say precisely what their role will be in asthma treatment, in the future. As with all medicines given by mouth, side effects are more likely than with inhaled medications. Rare liver cell injury, which disappeared when the drug was stopped, has been reported with one of these LTD_4 antagonists.

ALLERGY SHOTS (IMMUNOTHERAPY)

Allergy shots are believed to desensitize people against allergies. They can be useful in rhinitis. There is less evidence to suggest that allergy shots reduce the severity of asthma. Immunotherapy "shots" start with very dilute solutions of specific allergens, the strengths of which are gradually increased so that the body will produce blocking factors.

Some success has been reported in treating hay fever with ragweed pollen extract, and recently, evidence suggests that desensitization against grass pollen and cats may be helpful in asthma as well as in rhinitis. Overall, the lack of benefit is probably due to the fact that allergy is only one component of asthma; even in allergic asthma, many different allergens are usually involved. It would be necessary to desensitize against each one for a good effect. Injections are expensive and time consuming, and it is not known how long any benefit will last. The major disadvantage includes painful swelling of the arm at the site of injections and the occasional severe reaction. Several deaths have been reported in Sweden, and the Committee on Safety of Medicines in the

UK has advised doctors against using allergy shots. Even if allergy shots are of some benefit, there is little evidence to suggest that more than 2 or 3 years of treatment is of value, even for people with hay fever.

ANTIHISTAMINES

These medications are often available without prescription and include promethazine (Phenergan), chlorpheniramine (Chlor-Trimeton), Benadryl, and others. They block histamine and relieve allergic rhinitis (hay fever). These older antihistamines cause drowsiness.

The new generation of long-acting antihistamines include terfenadine* (Seldane), astemizole (Hismanal), loratidine (Claritin), and letirizine (Reactine). They do not cause drowsiness and may be given safely in higher than "average" doses. They do not reduce asthma symptoms but are safe for children with asthma to take for their manifestations of allergy.

ANTIBIOTICS

Antibiotics are useful only if your child has a bacterial infection (e.g., an ear infection) along with the asthma attack, or if there is evidence of pneumonia or sinus infection. Because children with asthma often have recurring episodes of cough, antibiotics are sometimes given repeatedly before it is realized that the yellow phlegm is not due to bacterial infection, but rather to eosinophils (the typical asthma cells), which give it the same appearance. Nevertheless, during some episodes of asthma, in addition to asthma therapy, bacterial infection can occur and antibiotics may be needed.

*Although these medications are effective, there have been occasional reports of abnormal heart rhythm in adult patients taking these long-acting antihistamines with other medications, notably some antibiotics. Therefore, it is important that you let your doctor and pharmacist know the names of other medications you are taking.

51

CHAPTER SEVEN

A LOGICAL AND SIMPLE APPROACH TO CONTROLLING ASTHMA AND TREATING ATTACKS

Most children with asthma can achieve excellent control of the condition and lead almost completely normal lives. The aim of treatment is always to have and maintain the best possible results.

AIMS OF TREATMENT

The main aims should be to

1. eliminate all identifiable causes, including allergens and trigger factors.
2. use medications in the minimum maintenance dose necessary to provide complete freedom from symptoms and normal (or best possible) pulmonary function.
3. anticipate and prevent asthma attacks by treating even moderate deterioration early and vigorously; usually by initiating or considerably increasing two- to fourfold the inhaled steroid dose.

ACHIEVING CONTROL OF YOUR CHILD'S ASTHMA

Good asthma control means that

1. your child is free of symptoms.
2. if symptoms do occur, they are mild and readily relieved by a bronchodilator puffer, which should be effective for at least 4 to 6 hours. (Short-acting bronchodilators required even once a day on a regular basis indicate poor control and the need for more anti-inflammatory medication.)
3. asthma should not interfere with your child's schooling or strenuous exercise, and must never awaken him or her from sleep.

4. your child will *not* require emergency department visits or hospitalization.
5. your child experiences no side effects from medications.
6. normal or near normal peak flow readings (or maintenance of the best possible result) are consistently maintained. Peak flow readings (if these are performed regularly) should not vary more than 10 to 15% from morning to night.

PRINCIPLES OF TREATMENT

1. Make the correct diagnosis of asthma and its severity.
2. Remove allergens and triggers as completely as possible from your child's environment and provide vigorous treatment to ensure you establish control quickly.
3. Give enough medication for a long enough period (usually three months or so) to achieve maximum improvement in symptoms and lung function. After this, medications can slowly be decreased to a level that will maintain control over symptoms and peak flow over the long term.
4. Develop an asthma action plan with your doctor so that *you* can control the condition, prevent episodes of deterioration, and treat most asthma attacks yourself.
5. Schedule regular follow-up visits with your child's doctor to make sure that things are going as well as possible, particularly if flare-ups occur.
6. Seek referral to a specialist knowledgeable in treating lung disease and allergies if the asthma is very severe, requires large doses of steroid aerosol, or asthma control cannot be achieved.
   (Remember that controlling the inflammation that causes asthma is far superior to simply treating the symptoms with bronchodilator puffers.)

At the start of the asthma treatment plan, your child may have a chest x–ray, allergy skin tests, breathing tests — before and after bronchodilator puffs — and possibly asthma provocation tests. You may be advised to purchase a peak flow meter. This will give your doctor information about the cause and severity of the asthma over a period (see Chapter 5).

Asthma, Exercise, and Scuba Diving

Although exercise is an important asthma trigger, children with asthma should continue to exercise. Asthma medication should be adjusted to facilitate activity. This is much better than trying to prevent asthma attacks by being inactive. However, asthmatics should *not* scuba dive because a small mucus plug could lead to over distention and rupture of air sacs during ascent and to a so-called *air embolism*, which could be life threatening. For the same reason, uncontrolled asthma can also make air travel dangerous because commercial airplane cabins are pressurized to 8000 ft. This can cause difficulty breathing for people who have low oxygen levels in their blood even at sea level.

Transient Allergen Exposures

Sometimes it is impossible to completely avoid allergens (e.g., you may visit a friend who has cats or dogs or who smokes). You can prevent or reduce the severity of the resulting asthma attack, nasal congestion, and itchy eyes by taking a long-acting antihistamine and inhaling 4 puffs of cromolyn or nedocromil along with 2 puffs of an inhaled bronchodilator at least 15 minutes before the exposure. The medication should be continued every 4 to 6 hours while the exposure persists. To prevent the inflammation associated with the late allergic reaction that might otherwise persist for 2 or 3 weeks, the dose of inhaled steroid should be doubled for 7 to 10 days after an intense exposure. Note that using extra inhaled steroid 10 to 15 minutes before exposure *will not* prevent the allergic reaction because this medicine takes about 2 to 3 hours to begin working.

LONG-TERM CONTROL OF ASTHMA

If avoidance procedures are successful (e.g., if your child is only allergic to cats and is no longer exposed to them) the asthma will be "cured" until exposure occurs again. Little or no medication may be required. This happy outcome will occur only if your child is allergic to just one or two easily avoided things.

Medications are required

1. to bring, and keep, asthma under control.
2. to treat flare-ups of asthma.
3. to prevent asthma attacks triggered by exercise or allergens.

The specific medications and dosage needed to control an attack depend on the severity of the asthma. Severity is largely measured by how much the asthma symptoms interfere with a child's life and the amount of preventer medication (e.g., inhaled steroids) needed to control the asthma. This is different from the acute attack that can occur in even mild asthmatics (severity level 1) under circumstances such as an exposure to a large amount of allergens, irritant chemicals, or a severe viral chest cold.

Defining Severity Levels

Severity Level 1: Well-controlled asthma   The child is free of symptoms; bronchodilators are needed three, or fewer, times a week; and lung function is normal.

Severity Level 2:   Symptoms are present from time to time on most days, but these are relieved by bronchodilators, which are required four or more times per week. The peak flow as measured at home is 10 to 20% below predicted or best achievable values. Peak flow is 15 to 25% lower in the morning than in the evening.

Severity Level 3:   Asthma symptoms occur frequently, interfere with exercise or sleep, and may cause wheezing and chest tightness. The bronchodilator is needed daily, and peak flow readings are 20 to 40% below the predicted or best achievable result. The variability in peak flow readings from morning to night is 25% or more.

Severity Level 4:   Asthma symptoms are present almost continuously. They do not completely disappear even after bronchodilator inhalation. The peak flow reading is 40 to 50% below normal (or best previously achievable).

In most children, increased symptoms, especially at night, and the need for bronchodilator puffs are the clearest indications of deterioration. In others, airway narrowing can become severe quickly, even before the child realizes that an attack is in progress. If your child can detect increasing symptoms, adjustments in medications are best related to symptoms and the need for increased bronchodilator puffs. If your child is over age 3 to 4, and deterioration is difficult to determine at an early stage, it may be wise to adjust the level of treatment to regularly measured peak flow. Use a peak flow meter with clearly indicated color coded zones that indicate severity (see page 60). Early intervention can usually ward off serious attacks.

MONITORING THERAPY

When asthma is first diagnosed, or at any time the asthma is not under control, diary cards that list symptoms, medications taken, and peak flow values provide an excellent method for following how well your child's asthma is being controlled. By noting any major allergen exposures or triggers on the diary card, you can help your doctor help your child. The diary card used at the Asthma Center for Children, at the Brenner Children's Hospital in Winston-Salem, North Carolina, is included in this book, and you can photocopy it for your child's use.

Children older than 3 to 5 years, who need daily asthma medications, should use a peak flow meter and take measurements first thing in the morning and at bed time. The test is easy to perform — your child takes the biggest possible breath in through the mouth and, then he or she exhales through the mouth only as quickly and completely as possible into the peak flow meter (like blowing out birthday candles). The best of three successive attempts should be recorded on the asthma diary card. Contact your doctor if the peak flow is steadily falling, even if symptoms do not increase. Newer peak flow meters help you to adjust the medication according to deterioration in peak flow, because they are clearly marked with green, yellow, and red zones. These zones are related to the best achievable values, so that your doctor can provide written instructions as to what to do should the peak flow fall. Early morning flow rates are usually the lowest of the day. The variation between morning and afternoon results is called *diurnal variability*, and it is normally less than 10 to 15%.

Our goal is to achieve **GREAT** asthma control — that is good asthma control on a *minimum* amount of medication. To achieve this, if your child is suffering a flare-up of asthma at the time treatment is started, you must first achieve good control by means of whatever medication is needed (including oral steroids).

Asthma Treatment According to Severity Levels (or to the Peak Flow Meter's Red, Yellow, and Green Zones)

Severity Level 1: Mild and infrequent asthma may sometimes require bronchodilators (no more than four times a week), usually before exposure to triggers such as exercise or cold air. Symptoms may be absent for weeks or months and are generally mild. Before exercise, 1 or 2 puffs of a shorter-acting bronchodilator often takes care of the problem. The long-acting bronchodilator, Serevent, at 1 or 2 puffs twice a day may provide effective protection against exercise-induced asthma. An alternative might be to use the Serevent one hour before exercise, but only if the exercise occurs intermittently.

Severity Level 2: Symptoms occur daily, but these are usually mild and rarely interfere with sleep or school. The mainstay of treatment are the anti-inflammatory preventer medications, such as a small dose of daily inhaled steroid at 2 to 4 puffs twice daily with a holding chamber. The bronchodilator inhaler should then be used "as needed." After 7 to 10 days of steroid treatment, the bronchodilator should be required only infrequently; peak flow should be near normal (or best achievable). Peak flow should vary from morning to night by less than 15%. If this is not happening, *a larger dose of inhaled steroid is needed*.

Cromolyn or nedocromil can sometimes be as effective as low-dose inhaled steroid. Some doctors prefer to start with cromolyn or nedocromil as an alternative to low-dose inhaled steroids. Pediatric asthma specialists generally prefer to begin with steroids so that the asthma can be quickly and safely brought under control and because preventer "monotherapy" with inhaled steroids makes adjustment of the medication during flare-ups easy to teach as the mainstay of an action plan. An important principle is to start with a relatively high dose that is continued for 6 to 8 weeks. Subsequently, a minimum maintenance dose is sought by reducing the dose gradually every 2 weeks.

Severity Level 3: Higher doses of inhaled steroids are required to control symptoms and achieve normal peak flow. While the steroids are controlling the inflammation, bronchodilators may be required four or more times a day. If asthma control remains poor, in spite of high doses of inhaled steroids taken twice daily, the same total dose may work better if given 3 or 4 times a day. With any inhaled steroid, MDI spacers or holding chambers should be used; accessory devices include spacers (no valves) and holding chambers with valves. If control remains poor in spite of careful environmental control, along with high doses of inhaled steroids and regular bronchodilators, and if you are sure that your child has been taking the prescribed doses of anti-inflammatory medications and has actually been inhaling the aerosol into the lungs, many asthma specialists recommend adding oral steroids to the treatment. Because this powerful anti-inflammatory medicine can cause side effects if taken for more than a few weeks at a time (as may be necessary with severe transient flare-ups), doctors are always careful to use the lowest possible dose to minimize side effects. In severe asthma, ipratropium (Atrovent) may help to restore asthma control. Theophylline may also be added on a trial basis, but it usually adds very little to symptom control.

Before adding regular oral steroids to your child's medications, you and your doctor should carefully review the diagnosis, current treatment, including drug doses and inhaler use, and factors that may potentially make it difficult to achieve control (e.g., environmental triggers, sinusitis, or gastroesophageal reflux).

Beginning and "Fine Tuning" Treatment

If at the time of your first visit to the doctor, your child's symptoms are bothersome, a few days of oral steroids (e.g., prednisone) may be given to help bring the asthma under control quickly. If doubling the inhaled steroid at the beginning of deterioration does not produce improvement within 12 to 24 hours, many doctors empower parents to deal with flare-ups by initiating short courses of prednisone themselves.

Once control is achieved, follow-up visits are gradually stretched out to 3 to 12 months. Attempts should be made to determine the lowest dose of medications that will maintain control. If "high" doses of inhaled steroids (approximately 500 µg beclomethasone per day) are not completely effective it is usually better to add a long-acting bronchodilator (eg., Serevent, Foradil) than to double the steroid.

Measuring peak flow is one of the best ways to guide therapy. If peak flow remains reduced by 15% or more below the child's best achievable result, *after bronchodilator puffs*, for more than two successive mornings, or if the peak flow falls into a higher severity level (yellow zone) in spite of attempts to correct deterioration by doubling the inhaled steroid puffs, a short course of prednisone may be needed to restore control. If the peak flow falls into the red zone, and does not immediately improve with bronchodilator puffs and rise into the yellow or green zone, prednisone should be started. In such situations, you should contact your doctor or go the nearest emergency department immediately.

Finding the Minimum Maintenance Dose

If the asthma has been well controlled for 2 to 3 months at a given level of treatment, you should discuss with your doctor the possibility of gradually reducing the amount of anti-inflammatory medication. This gradual reduction can continue until symptoms begin to recur, the peak flow begins to decrease, or an increased need for bronchodilator puffs is noted. In some children, the anti-inflammatory medications need to be continued over the long term, perhaps indefinitely. Children with allergic triggers may need continuous treatment only during the allergy season and for a short time afterwards. These children may also be advised to start their anti-inflammatory medication just before the beginning of the allergy season and taper the dose over the four weeks after the season is over. Control of asthma over the long term is the key to preventing severe attacks. Regular effective anti-inflammatory treatment may, over several months, produce a fundamental improvement in the disease, the opening of previously plugged airways, and a decrease in the need for medications. Tight control of asthma is also likely to prevent permanent damage to the airways. *Note: Never* discontinue your child's *preventer* (anti-inflammatory) medication without your doctor's specific instructions because a bad asthma attack could result.

Treating Asthma Flare-Ups

Despite attempts to maintain good control, asthma attacks might occur if your child is exposed to a large dose of allergens, certain food preservatives to which your child may be sensitive, or viral infections like the "flu." Very high air pollution levels may also trigger an asthma attack. You should have

TABLE 7–1   A Typical Asthma Plan

A. To Relieve Breathlessness Rapidly

1. Using a holding chamber (see Chapter 9), give two puffs of bronchodilator (e.g., albuterol/salbutamol) and wait about 5 minutes. If little or no improvement occurs, give four more puffs — one every
30 seconds. If after 5 minutes there has been little or no improvement,
give one additional bronchodilator puff each minute (to a maximum of
12 to 15 puffs) until the breathlessness is relieved or there is noticeable
trembling, whichever comes first. If necessary this procedure can be
repeated every 20 to 30 minutes for severe asthma. If improvement has
not occurred after a maximum of 15 puffs, your child should be given
steroid pills as prescribed and quickly taken to the emergency department. If your child is having a severe attack, you can give the puffs on
the way to the hospital. If you have a peak flow meter you can expect
an improvement of about 50% after giving the bronchodilator puffs. If
this works, as it usually does, proceed to Section B. If it does not work
call your doctor and go to the hospital emergency department!

2. If rapid deterioration is occurring, carry out the above on your way to
the hospital.

B. To Restore Control

1. Double the preventer medication (e.g., cromolyn, nedocromil, or
inhaled steroids). For example, if your child is already taking 2 puffs
4 times daily, increase to 4 puffs 4 times daily.

2. If doubling the preventer puffs produces no noticeable improvement
after 12 to 24 hours, or if there is continued worsening, oral steroid
(prednisone) should be started as written in your action plan. The dose
is determined by the weight of your child (usually about 0.5 to 1 mg
per pound, once each day). You will maintain this dose until peak flow
returns to the previous best values — usually within 5 to 7 days. You
should notify your doctor that you have started prednisone.

3. Make sure that you understand how quickly you should reduce the
dose of prednisone and what maintenance dose may be needed if necessary. Usual treatment is one half of the first week's dose for a second
week. Then the prednisone can usually be discontinued and the child
can continue with inhaled steroids as before. Children with severe and
unstable asthma may need long-term prednisone along with inhaled
steroids in high enough doses to keep the need for prednisone to an
absolute minimum.

a *written* action plan worked out with your doctor for dealing with these flare-ups and restoring control.

Using Action Plans   The action plan should incorporate all of the principles outlined above. The plan should be prepared in advance with your doctor and take into account your child's symptoms, the need for increased bronchodilator, or instructions about what to do should a fall in peak flow of more than 20% below your child's previous best (yellow zone) occur even after 4 puffs of bronchodilator have been given.

The action plan in action is a recipe for successful treatment of most asthma attacks. A typical action plan (which should be individualized by your doctor for your child) appears on the inside back cover. The example assumes that you have bronchodilators on hand and that your child's asthma is well controlled on inhaled preventers (anti-inflammatory medication).

Action Plan Not Working?   If the action plan has not started to work within 6 to 12 hours, if your child is gasping for breath, if the bronchodilator puffer works for less than 2 to 3 hours, or if the peak flow is decreased by 40 to 50% (red zone) and stays there after 4 puffs of bronchodilator, then you should immediately give your child prednisone (15–50 mg according to weight), give the bronchodilator (see above), contact your doctor, and go to the emergency department.

Implementing the Action Plan Using Peak Flow   This plan can be used if your child regularly uses a peak flow meter. Suppose that the best peak flow was 500 L per minute (for an adult-sized teenager), and for two morning readings taken 24 hours apart, the peak flow after using the bronchodilator inhaler is less than:

1. 400 (80% of the best reading) — double the dose of inhaled steroid and continue at the new level until readings are again within 90% of the previous best (450 or above). This will usually occur within 3 to 5 days.
2. 300 (60% of the best reading) — you should start oral prednisone until readings are again within 90% (this will usually take 3 to 7 days).
3. 250 (50% of best reading) — take the oral prednisone, follow instructions detailed under A above (To Relieve Breathlessness Rapidly), and go to the hospital emergency department after contacting your doctor.

Be prepared! Make copies of the action plan and keep them available in a prominent place at home, for teachers at school, and anywhere that your child is likely to spend time. Keep the necessary medications available at all times so that you or other care-givers can carry out the action plan. You should always have a spare supply of bronchodilator inhalers so that you do not run out in an emergency. These should be kept at home, at school, and with your child.

Note: Don't forget to take all of the medications and the aerosol holding chamber with you when you go on vacation!

Special Treatment Measures

Since the development of the valved holding chamber, nebulizers that use liquid drug solutions are rarely needed. They are expensive and inefficient. In the past, nebulizers were thought to be better for relieving severe asthma, but we know now that it was just a question of dose — much more medication was given by nebulizer than was contained in the 2 or 3 puffs usually given by MDI (puffer). Nevertheless, although bronchodilator puffs can almost always be repeated to the point of relief, occasionally children with very severe and unpredictable asthma may benefit from a home nebulizer system.

Bronchodilators are not a substitute for treating or preventing deterioration by increasing the dose of inhaled steroids or using short courses of oral steroids. Temporary relief is almost always obtained with a nebulizer containing a large dose of bronchodilator, but if bronchodilators are used repeatedly day after day without anti-inflammatory medications, the underlying inflammation and symptoms of asthma gradually get worse. Reliever medications (Proventil, Ventolin) **alone** should never be relied on to deal with a flare-up of asthma that is **severe**. Such attacks almost always require physician–supervised treatment and anti-inflammatory medications, especially prednisone.

Follow-up Visits with Your Child's Doctor

Follow-up visits are extremely important to assess your child's asthma control and adjust medications accordingly. If things are going well, such visits can be infrequent, but they should occur at least once a year so that your child can take advantage of any new therapy. If things are not going well, you should implement the action plan and arrange for your child to see the doctor as soon as possible!

With time, you and your child will become expert at self-care and be better able to manage and *prevent* frightening asthma attacks. The information in this book is intended to empower you to undertake care of your child's asthma or to enable an older child to become confident in achieving self-care.

A medical summary card is included inside the back cover of this book — you can copy it and ask your doctor to help you fill it out so that you can carry the action plan with you at all times. If a pencil is used, the card can be changed as medication is adjusted. Show the card to any doctor who cares for your child.

Changing from Long-Term Oral Steroids to Aerosol Steroids: A Word of Caution

As you know, many possible side effects are associated with the long-term use of oral steroids. One of the most important is suppression of your child's own cortisone (steroid) production. Fortunately, high-dose steroids taken by mouth can nearly always be replaced with much safer inhaled steroids. The transition to the inhaled medications should involve a *very* gradual reduction of the steroid tablets to allow the suppressed adrenal glands to recover and begin producing steroids once more. Then the transition can be made safely (monitored by measuring your child's serum cortisol levels). Nevertheless, for a period of 3 to 5 years, it should be assumed that these glands cannot produce sufficient cortisone at times of serious medical illness or surgery, and steroid supplements should be given. This is a good reason for wearing a Medic-Alert bracelet. If your child has been taking oral steroids for 3 to 6 months, they should be gradually tapered for several months before being discontinued. If your child has been on oral steroids six months or more,

1. the dose should be decreased very gradually under a doctor's supervision.
2. your child should wear a Medic-Alert bracelet, indicating that he or she is on long-term steroid therapy.
3. you should tell all doctors caring for your child that your child took oral steroids for a long term.
4. you should keep oral steroids on hand, so that if your child develops symptoms of severe asthma or steroid withdrawal (weakness, dizziness, vomiting), you can start a dose of oral steroids as advised by your doctor.

As oral steroids are discontinued, the side effects will steadily decrease.

COST OF ASTHMA THERAPY

Although this book is intended to give you the best information about the treatment of asthma, we are well aware that the best asthma treatment can be expensive, especially for severe cases. The cost must be considered in the light of the benefits that result. Fortunately for most children with asthma, anti-inflammatory treatment with inhaled steroids is a fairly inexpensive way to control asthma effectively. The anti-inflammatory medications also make the need for bronchodilators much less. The average daily cost of controlling asthma in most children (excluding the 5% with very severe asthma, who require high doses of multiple medications) should be less than half the daily cost of the average smoker's cigarette consumption.

TREATING ANAPHYLACTIC REACTIONS

If your child has anaphylactic reactions (severe allergy accompanied with hives and breathlessness), you should have adrenaline (epinephrine) autoinjection syringes or keep an epinephrine puffer readily available (Primatene). Primatene is available in the United States without prescription and is inexpensive. Because of its 30-minute duration of action and the possibility of serious side effects with regular use, Primatene should *not* be used to treat asthma. However, these same side effects make adrenaline inhalers like Primatene useful for treating anaphylactic reactions. An anaphylactic reaction should be treated by inhaling as many puffs as necessary to produce a sensation of trembling (usually 10 to 15 puffs) and relief of breathlessness. This can be repeated every 20 to 30 minutes, if necessary, on your way to the hospital. If these are readily available, an antihistamine and prednisone should also be given before leaving for the hospital.

CHAPTER EIGHT

EMERGENCY DEPARTMENT AND HOSPITAL TREATMENT OF SEVERE ASTHMA

If your child's asthma is very severe, and there has not been a good response to increased treatment within a few hours, or if there is steady deterioration, you should take your child to the emergency department or to your doctor. If your child is very short of breath, has blue lips or tongue, or is very agitated and pale, call your doctor and leave a message to say that you are on your way to the hospital. Children with asthma should be taken to the hospital quickly if

1. they are severely ill, look blue, and thus need oxygen.
2. they do not seem to be getting better with treatment at home, or are getting worse.
3. they live some distance away from the hospital, and transportation would not be available if they got worse.

If early treatment is instituted, death from asthma is very rare. Children treated in the emergency department, who show considerable improvement, are usually sent home with oral steroids for 1 to 2 weeks, and early follow-up is arranged. Doubling the dose of inhaled steroid is the usual maintenance therapy given for 2 to 3 weeks after the prednisone is discontinued.

Depending on the severity, your child may be admitted to the pediatric ward or even to the intensive care unit for closer observation. A severe attack makes the effort of breathing like breathing through a narrow drinking straw. The chest muscles become exhausted, and not enough oxygen gets into the blood. These problems are caused by marked narrowing of the airways by swelling, constriction of the smooth muscle in the walls, and mucus plugging.

Often treatment brings about a marked and rapid improvement. If this does not happen, and your child becomes increasingly exhausted, it may be necessary to put a thin plastic tube into your child's windpipe and assist breathing with a machine called a ventilator. Since the initial treatment described in Chapter 7 is usually effective this is rarely necessary.

A life-threatening asthma attack needs **IMMEDIATE ATTENTION**.

GETTING TO THE HOSPITAL

As part of the action plan, you and your doctor should work out how a severe episode will be handled. When in doubt about the severity of your child's asthma, call your doctor or take your child to the nearest hospital emergency department, preferably at a hospital that has expertise in caring for sick children. Depending on the severity of the asthma, you can drive your child to the hospital yourself, take a taxi, or if the child appears severely ill, call an ambulance. If the ambulance cannot come at once, call the police or fire department. Get your child to the nearest hospital as quickly as possible by any means available.

The Hospital Emergency Department

If your child is *extremely* ill, (s)he will be seen at once by a nurse and/or doctor, and treatment will be started. Show your child's doctor the medical summary card (see inside back cover), even without being asked for it.

Emergency Department Treatment

The doctor will talk to you briefly to find out the background to your child's attack, do a quick physical examination, while at the same time, usually starting the following treatment:

1. Provision of oxygen, with monitoring of blood oxygen levels by means of an oximeter (a light that shines through your child's finger).
2. With children over six years of age a breathing test (pulmonary function test) may be tried, but if your child is very ill, this probably will not be done. Bring the child's peak flow meter and diary cards with you to the hospital as well as all the medications to show the doctor.
3. Your child will be given puffs of bronchodilator (if you have not already done this to the point of shakiness). Although in many emergency departments, bronchodilators are still given using a nebulizer, in many centers (including the emergency departments in the USA, Canada, and England, where the authors of this book work) puffers are used with valved holding chambers. Even in the emergency department this provides rapid and safe asthma therapy with fewer side effects. Bronchodilators in high doses will provide rapid partial relief of the breathlessness. If your child uses a puffer with a holding chamber at home, bring these with you to the hospital also. If improvement occurs rapidly, it may not be necessary to give oral steroids. Except for less severe attacks, most children are given oral steroids for 3 to 7 days to ensure steady recovery. Until the oral or intravenous steroids begin to work in 3 to 6 hours, it may be necessary to give large doses of beta-agonist bronchodilators (albuterol/salbutamol) every 30 to 60 minutes.

Your child will usually improve on this treatment, and you will then be sent home with instructions to increase the dose of anti-inflammatory treatment if your child is taking preventers. A follow-up visit should be arranged to see your child's own doctor within a few days. The whole asthma treatment program should be re-evaluated by your doctor to try and prevent similar episodes in the future.

Hospital Admission

If deterioration continues; if your child was admitted to hospital within the last few weeks and has been taking oral steroids at home recently; if only minimal improvement in peak flow occurs, despite many bronchodilator puffs; or if you are afraid to take your child home because previous similar episodes showed progressive deterioration, the doctor is likely to admit your child to hospital for close observation and additional treatment with oral steroids. The expectation is that improvement will be rapid, and your child will be home again within a few days.

RECOVERING FROM SEVERE ATTACKS

Well-controlled asthma should rarely result in attacks; however, even so-called "mild" asthma of severity Level 1 can sometimes become severe with a flu-like illness or after exposure to very large amounts of allergens. The duration of treatment required for recovery is approximately equal to the time that the asthma flare-up was present before treatment was started; so it is important that with the *onset* of deterioration vigorous treatment be started as soon as possible.

It is a good idea to review the asthma management and treatment plans periodically with your doctor to make sure that you are doing everything possible to maintain good asthma control over the long term and that the smallest possible dose of inhaled steroid and other medications are being used. Bring all medications to every follow-up visit with your doctor and make sure that you, or your child, *always* have adequate supplies of medications to deal with any conceivable situation. This is *especially important when your child is away from home, at camp, or on vacation.*

AEROSOL INHALERS, METERED DOSE INHALER ACCESSORY DEVICES, NEBULIZERS, AND OXYGEN

The best way to control asthma is to take inhaled anti-inflammatory medications regularly, and bronchodilators as required. The best, most versatile, and least expensive treatment is the metered dose inhaler usually used together with a valved aerosol holding chamber. Other delivery systems include dry powder inhalers from which your child sucks in the medication — these probably should not be used in children under age 6 — and nebulizers containing the drug solution, which is delivered with gas pressure from a compressor (jet nebulizer) or by ultrasonic nebulizer.

METERED DOSE INHALERS AND HOW TO USE THEM

These little aerosol cans provide a precise dose of medication with each puff, but because the spray comes out fairly quickly, children under the age of 5 or 6 may have trouble

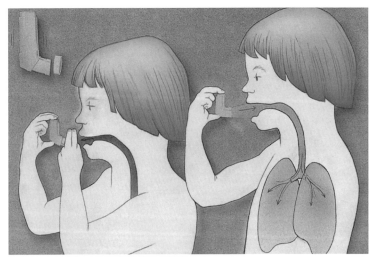

Figure 9–1. How to take a metered dose inhaler. Upper left: the cap has been removed from the MDI. Lower left: a child holds the inhaler about 1.5 inches from the open mouth. On the right, the aerosol has been discharged and is being inhaled into the lungs.

coordinating aerosol discharge with inhalation. For treatment to be effective, the aerosol must get into your child's lungs. The best use of an MDI involves five easy steps which you should review with your doctor and pharmacist. With older children (8 and above) no difficulty should be apparent, but younger children should have their treatment supervised by a parent.

How to Use an MDI

1. Remove the cap and shake vigorously 5 to 6 times.
2. Hold the inhaler firmly with mouthpiece about two finger-widths (4 cm) in front of your child's wide-open mouth. Direct the spray toward the back of the throat.
3. Your child can be taught to breathe out in a relaxed way as though completing a sigh (there is no need to exhale fully).
4. As a slow deep breath is gradually taken, the canister of the aerosol should be pushed down to release the medication, which is then drawn down into the lungs during the 5 or 6 seconds it takes to inhale fully (like the beginning of a big sigh). The canister should only be pushed once for each breath.
5. Your child should then hold his or her breath for up to 10 seconds before exhaling.
6. Additional puffs should be given one at a time about 10 to 20 seconds apart until your child has taken the total number prescribed by your doctor.

An alternative method of inhaling from an MDI is to place the inhaler mouthpiece between the closed lips and follow the same directions. The open-mouth method, however, delivers about twice as much medication to the lungs, and is therefore the one that we prefer.

If repeated attempts to use the inhaler are not very successful, or if your child is taking inhaled steroids, an accessory device such as the AeroChamber, Inspirease or Volumatic

Figure 9–2. AeroChamber with mask being used to administer MDI-generated aerosol therapy to an infant a few days old and a toddler aged 18 months.

should be used with the MDI. Such devices target *more aerosol* to the lungs reliably and so save money in the long run (see below). They also reduce steroid side effects.

New MDI Systems

Freon is the trade name for chemicals used until recently in air conditioners, refrigerators, foaming systems, and medication MDIs. Because of a worldwide concern about ozone depletion by these chlorofluorocarbons (CFCs), their use is being completely phased out over the next few years. Currently, CFCs can *only* be used in MDIs until replacement substances are widely available.

The 3M Riker company scientists have developed a beta-agonist bronchodilator (salbutamol) inhaler (Aeromir) and will soon introduce a steroid inhaler that is pressurized with the new propellant hydrofluroalkane (HFA 134a). It is as effective as CFC Ventolin (or Proventil), but has no ozone-depleting effect. Other companies are also developing similar formulations, which will replace the CFCs used in all medication MDIs in coming years.

Autohaler

This device, developed by the 3M Riker company is a mechanical unit that delivers medication on inhalation after the device is cocked. This device solves the coordination problem, and because only a very gentle inhalation is required to trigger it, children over age 6, elderly people, and even those having a severe attack can almost always get their aerosol medication reliably. This device does not replace the regular inhaler and holding chamber, however, because it is not able to reduce the throat dose of medication, which is the same as that used with the regular MDI or powder inhaler.

Metered Dose Inhaler Accessory (add-on) Devices

When an MDI is used, about 15% of the medication goes into the lungs, but the larger particles stay in the throat (pharynx) and plastic actuator (85%), where they are of no value in treatment, but can contribute to side effects. This problem has been addressed by simple devices that selectively removes large particles and decreases the throat dose about tenfold while slightly increasing the lung dose . These devices include AeroChamber, Inspirease, and Volumatic, which are supplied with a mouthpiece for older children, and the AeroChamber with masks of different sizes for infants, toddlers, and children. Holding chambers make it easier to coordinate puffing with inhaling and ensure that the aerosol gets into the lungs. Additional benefits of the accessory devices are reducing of the side effects due to medications depositing in the mouth including the unpleasant taste of inhaler medication; decreasing irritation of the throat, cough and hoarseness of the voice; and the almost complete elimination of the risk of a yeast infection called thrush, in the mouth and throat. Thrush is recognizable as curdy white patches inside the cheeks. If your child is on inhaled steroids, oral steroids, and antibiotics, and complains of a sore mouth and throat when swallowing, check for thrush. Thrush is easily treated and is not usually serious, but it can be prevented by using an accessory device.

Detailed instructions for the use of each of these accessory devices is enclosed with the device, and these should be read and followed carefully. The AeroChamber for infants and children comes with masks of graded sizes that fit the face. A tight fit is necessary or the medication will not be delivered with each breath. For maximum benefit from all of these devices, the static electricity charge that develops on most plastics should be eliminated. This is easily done by washing the device in dishwashing detergent about once every two weeks.

Accessory devices should not be used with the Autohaler. Accessory devices are now being specially designed for use with the CFC-free inhalers mentioned above.

Powder Inhalers

Dry powder inhalers (DPIs including Rotahaler, Ventadisk, Beclodisk, Spinhaler, Turbuhaler, Diskus, Clickhaler*) deliver powder particles of medication when the child inhales quickly. Because of the fast inhalation, most of the medication is deposited in the back of the throat as it is with an MDI, and as yet an add-on device to remove the particles that may cause side effects is not available. Such devices are under development.

Sometimes children under the age of 6 cannot inhale forcefully enough to get a full dose of medication from DPIs, especially during asthma attacks. With high-dose inhaled steroids, the total body dose is higher than with an MDI and a holding chamber. If your child blows into the DPI unit before inhaling, the medicine will be dispersed, and because of the humidity blown into the device, the next 3 or 4 doses may not be very effective either. As with any aerosol devices, careful instruction should be provided by your doctor and pharmacist. You should

*Not yet available in the United States

not leave your doctor's office until you have been shown exactly how to load the medicine and observed your child inhaling the powder reliably.

Small-Volume Wet Nebulizers

Small-volume wet nebulizers may work by air pressure (compressor or cylinder) or electronically (ultrasonic). They have been largely replaced by valved holding chamber devices for home and hospital. Some children "prefer" the nebulizer. Also, new and experimental medications are usually first given by a nebulizer.

Disadvantages of nebulizers include the need for a power source, and compressors. Ultrasonics vary considerably in efficiency and dose delivered. There is also the possibility of contamination of poorly maintained nebulizers, and relatively low efficiency compared to MDIs or DPIs, so that much larger doses of the medication are required to get an equivalent effect. Because of this, medications given this way are associated with greater costs and a greater risk of side effects. Not all drugs available in MDIs are available for use with nebulizers. This is a particular deficiency with respect to inhaled steroids in the USA. In some countries, a budesonide suspension suitable for use with jet (but not ultrasonic) nebulizers is available. It is expensive and less efficient than MDI puffers and holding chambers fitted with masks for treating infants. The ultrasonic nebulizers currently available have been shown to be more expensive and even less effective than jet nebulizers. We do not recommend their use.

Oxygen Therapy in Asthma: When, Why, and How?

In contrast to older people with chronic bronchitis and emphysema, who may require oxygen at night or during exercise, children with asthma rarely need to keep oxygen at home since it would be required very rarely during severe life-threatening attacks. The amount of oxygen needed under

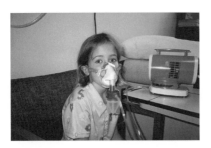

Figure 9–3. Small volume jet nebulizer providing bronchodilator therapy by means of a mask. The large device is the air compressor that drives the nebulizer.

those circumstances is the amount that will restore near normal levels in the blood (greater than 0.93 oxygen saturation). Rarely, if you live far away from an emergency department, and your child gets severe and unpredictable asthma attacks despite maximum treatment and careful monitoring, keeping oxygen at hand may be advisable, for use on the way to the hospital.

SMOKING

Asthmatics should never become smokers, because smoking can lead to severe and progressive damage to the air passages, such as chronic bronchitis and emphysema. This is also true of marijuana, and is a good example of "adding insult to injury." Parents should never smoke in the vicinity of their asthmatic children, either! Recently, it was shown that mothers who smoke during pregnancy, while nursing, or who expose their children to environmental tobacco smoke, may predispose their children to asthma later on.

Every attempt should be made to control a child's asthma so well that, except for taking medication as needed, the child leads a completely normal life. With good asthma control, children should rarely miss school or gym class. Children with asthma should be able to participate in all sports (except scuba diving). Swimming is a particularly good activity because exercise-associated asthma is less likely in warm humid air. However, high chlorine levels in some swimming pools, or mold in poorly maintained pool areas, can trigger asthma attacks, especially if asthma control is poor.

Some children are embarrassed to use their inhalers in school. This situation may be worsened if they have to get the medication from their teacher or school nurse before using it. Children who do so at home should keep the inhaler with them. Teachers should know, however, that a child has asthma and be given reading material so that they can help if an attack occurs during the school day. Your doctor should write to the school requesting that an older child (age 6 and over) control their own inhaler use. A sample letter is included at the end of this chapter.

Teenagers can be difficult to treat because they sometimes want to deny that they have a chronic problem, and when they are feeling reasonably well, "forget" to take their medication.

Ideally, a "hot line" should be available at treatment centers so that patients or referring physicians can contact an asthma specialist at any time for assistance and referral.

Children may try to manipulate their parents and teachers by playing up their asthma, even to the point of faking attacks. The child who hates gym class may "conveniently" develop an attack before or during the class each day.

"Asthma" may be used as an excuse to avoid taking examinations or even for skipping school. This is attention-seeking behavior, and should be discouraged because it can lead to more abnormal behavior. If the child gets a lot of sympathy, being an asthmatic may be transformed into a "pleasant" experience, thereby encouraging illness-related acting-out behavior. This can lead to the unnecessary administration of increasing doses of medication, including oral steroids with their attendant side effects. It might also make it difficult to tell when the child is really sick. If you suspect that your child is "acting out" mention it to your doctor. Simple peak flow tests (highly variable on repeat tests if the child is "faking" it) can usually distinguish between asthma that is not under good control from the pseudo-asthma of a child seeking attention.

EXERCISE

Play and vigorous exercise are one of the best parts of being a child. Bronchodilator aerosols can be taken before exercise to prevent exercise-associated asthma, which occurs even in those with otherwise well-controlled asthma. Preventative puffs of beta agonist, alone or with Intal, taken about 15 minutes before exercise may prevent the problem. An asthmatic child can undertake virtually any sport but scuba diving. Depending upon their allergies to animals, asthmatic children should probably avoid sports such as horseback riding and careers such as veterinary medicine.

After a severe attack, heavy exercise should be limited until lung function tests, as well as symptoms, have returned to near normal. One of the most important goals of asthma therapy is to keep the condition under tight control so that children can exercise well. A number of successful Olympic athletes are asthmatic and so are many professional hockey, baseball, and football players!

COPING WITH ASTHMA

How should you cope with asthma in your child? The most direct answer is that you should treat your son or daughter as you would a *normally healthy child*. With proper treatment, asthma can almost always be controlled so that children can do almost everything as well as their peers.

LEARNING TO TAKE MEDICATIONS

Children should become actively involved in their own care, and this includes their measuring and recording peak flow and taking medications as soon as they are able to. Most children and adolescents must be supervised to some extent, and under age 13, it is unlikely that the child will be able to take full responsibility for taking medications for asthma self-care. Leaving it to the child or teenager to decide if they really "need" to take their preventer medicine is a recipe for disaster. As a parent, you must supervise treatment to make sure that the younger child is using the inhalers correctly and as prescribed. Many of the inhaled anti-inflammatory medications and the newer long-acting bronchodilators are taken twice a day. Linking the use of the inhaler with brushing teeth in the morning and at night is a good idea. Periodically review the older child's peak flow diary with them and discuss their treatment plan in the light of the peak flow results, particularly if they are showing asthma symptoms. In teenagers, poor asthma control can result from exposure to high levels of allergens (e.g., dogs and cats), failure to take the full dose of preventer medication regularly, or sometimes smoking.

To check whether your child is actually taking the full dose of medication prescribed, it helps to know approximately how long each preventer inhaler should last, if used regularly. The number of puffs available is written on each canister, and since you know how many puffs a day should be taken, you can easily predict how many days the inhaler is likely to last. You can mark the date when the child started a new canister on the label. If the canister lasts fewer days, then the medication is being overused, and if it lasts longer, then doses are being "forgotten." For example, your child started a new canister on the label, and your child should be taking two puffs of Vanceril twice a day; if there are 200 puffs in the canister, then each MDI should last about 50 days or 7 weeks. If at the end of 2 months, a lot of medication remains in the canister (you can tell by shaking or placing it in a glass full of water, you know that your child has been missing many doses.

Similarly, you should be aware if your child is overusing the bronchodilator inhaler. This indicates either that the asthma is out of control, and that higher doses of inhaled anti-inflammatory medication should be used, or that your child is wasting medication by discharging the canister playfully. Early recognition of bronchodilator overuse is a good way to detect that asthma is out of control before a serious attack occurs. For example, a Ventolin inhaler contains 200 puffs. If your child is supposed to take two puffs before exercise and additional puffs only as needed, and you find that you need to refill the prescription every three weeks, your child is taking nine puffs a day — which is too much for well-controlled asthma.

Asthma control should become as much an easy and routine part of life as good dental care. When this happens, your child will have taken control of his or her asthma, and you will find that the fear of asthma no longer controls you or your child.

CHOOSING A DOCTOR

While the information in this book will empower you to become an active partner in the management of your child's asthma, no book can ever replace the working relationship that you can develop with your child's doctor and/or asthma specialist. Family doctors, pediatricians, allergists, and lung specialists (pulmonologists) are all aware of the importance of anti-inflammatory treatment and the importance of avoiding allergens and triggers. They are also usually aware of the newer medications and new delivery devices that can help children use the aerosol medications most effectively. In a good asthma treatment center, your child's doctor or assistant should take the time to explain, teach, and answer questions about asthma.

Many larger cities have good asthma treatment centers, particularly centers that are a part of medical schools. It is a good idea, particularly if your child has severe asthma, to consult a specialist who works in a medical school. He can then provide your own doctor with additional information that might help to improve your child's quality of life.

Many teaching hospitals provide opportunities for you and your child to assist with research projects that are looking into the causes and treatments of asthma. It was only with the help of people like you who helped with the testing of new medications that safe and effective asthma therapy is now available for most children.

ASTHMA IN BABIES

Even babies can sometimes develop asthma. It tends to develop if there is a family history of asthma, if they were born prematurely and needed mechanical ventilation in the intensive care unit, if they have eczema, if they have had respiratory syncytial virus (RSV) disease or bronchiolitis, or if they are frequently exposed to tobacco smoke. RSV is a common virus that affects almost all infants and children during the first two years of life. It is present mainly in the winter. Infants can have the smallest airways affected by an inflammatory condition called bronchiolitis often caused by RSV. These infants develop wheezing and breathlessness and have a 50% chance of developing asthma. This risk can be reduced by

1. avoiding smoking in the vicinity of the infant.
2. never giving bottles in bed. This is because they may choke on milk (aspirate) when they fall asleep, it can also lead to an increased risk of ear infections.
3. decreasing exposure to allergens and irritants as much as possible by not having humidity over 35% in the bedroom. This is because moisture encourages the growth of molds and house dust mites which worsen the asthma. Vaporizers and humidifiers should not be used in a child's bedroom. Some doctors have shown benefit in using a *dehumidifier* during the day to prevent mite growth. Mites can also be effectively eliminated by putting your child's pillow and plush toys in the freezer once every week or so, for about 12 hours. Although this kills the mites, it will not eliminate their antigens. Antigens in house dust can only be reduced by careful cleaning.

Warning: Using chest rubs like Vicks or placing Vaseline inside the infants nose will not improve rhinitis or asthma and could cause serious lung problems if inhaled. They should not be used in children with asthma.

Asthma in babies can be difficult to diagnose and treat, and repeated courses of antibiotics may be given for "bronchitis" before it is appreciated that asthma is the real problem. The nose is often congested ("snotty nose"), and secretions can be collected and sent to be examined for eosinophil cells. If the mucus has a large number of eosinophils in it, it will look yellow, just as though infection were present. This finding suggests that the runny nose is due to asthma rather than to infection and indicates that anti-inflammatory treatment for rhinitis and asthma should be given — instead of antibiotics — probably over the long-term to prevent flare-ups.

Many pediatricians are conservative and continue to use nebulizers instead of MDIs and valved holding chambers. Nebulizers are comparatively expensive, cumbersome, inefficient, and difficult to carry around. They can be time-consuming for preparing and administering medications. If babies cry through the 10 to 15 minutes needed to give the medicine with a nebulizer, they get very little. Most of it is wasted into the room. Steroids should only be given by MDI and a holding chamber unless for some reason this is not possible.

As indicated earlier, some babies have symptoms due to inborn (congenital) abnormalities of the airway, which can lead to wheezing and increased respiratory distress particularly after inhaling bronchodilator medications which therefore should not be given to them.

Asthma, Day-Care, and Baby-sitters
Since infants or children in day-care are frequently exposed to respiratory infections — the number-one trigger of asthma in this age group and which account for about two-thirds of all asthma attacks — they are far more likely to develop asthma. Private day-care in homes can also expose the child to tobacco smoke, pets, house dust mites, and molds. A busy day-care center may not have the time to carefully monitor and treat the asthmatic infant. A letter similar to the one for the school nurse (see page 86), the asthma care plan, and the necessary medications should be given to the day-care center. Care-givers should know how to obtain medical assistance and how to recognize when an infant needs help. They should know that asthma is not contagious,

and be willing to reduce the level of allergens and irritants in the environment for your child (and for the other children). Your baby-sitter will need this information, and if the child's custody is shared between two parents, sets of medications and copies of the treatment plan should be available in both homes. Both parents should understand how to initiate increased asthma treatment early during flare-ups to prevent severe attacks.

SAMPLE LETTER TO THE SCHOOL NURSE (DOCTOR)

Date:
To the teacher and school nurse of _____
                                              student name

Name of Doctor:
Doctor's Office Telephone Number:
Doctor's Pager/Exchange:
This student has asthma. The medication for this that must be taken regularly includes:

Medication Name	Dose	Time to Take
[1]		
[2]		
[3]		
[4]		

It is recommended that for the regularly taken medication the student (check one)
[ ]   can take the medication without supervision
[ ]   should take medication with the help of a teacher or the school nurse
When used as directed, this medication should have no significant side effects, except:
[ ]   mild tremor (with bronchodilators)
[ ]   other:
If the asthma is under good control, no exercise restrictions should be observed. However, during pollen season, cold weather, and after an respiratory infection, asthma may be worsened by exercise. To prevent this, the student should take the following medication at least 15 minutes before exercising:
_____

Symptoms of a serious asthma attack include breathlessness, chest tightness, wheezing, and difficulty talking.
If the student is using a peak flow meter, his or her best peak flow reading is usually: _____.
Mild asthma symptoms should be associated with a peak flow reading of: _____ to _____.
A severe attack would have a reading below: _____.

For a mild attack the student should do the following:

For a severe attack the student and the school nurse should do the following:
Please call me if you have any questions about the care of asthma or the medications.

CHAPTER ELEVEN

NOSES, SINUSES, EYES, EARS, AND ASTHMA

Allergy is caused by a tendency of the body's immune system to over-react to certain inhaled and ingested substances. Exactly how this happens is unknown. However, even in identical twins, if one twin has asthma, the chance that the other twin will develop the condition is only about 30%. If your family has a strong history of allergy, you should take a careful decision about getting domestic pets, particularly cats, to which your child could become sensitized.

Allergies affect not only the lungs, but also the nose (rhinitis, nasal polyps), sinuses (sinusitis), eyes (conjunctivitis), and skin (atopic dermatitis or eczema). Children with atopic dermatitis are much more likely to get rhinitis or asthma. Treatment of allergy-related symptoms in these organs is based on reducing allergens to an absolute minimum, just as with asthma. The medications used are also similar and involve using anti-inflammatory agents in the nose and eyes during the allergy season, and, year round, if the symptoms are continuous. Nasal steroids include Flonase, Rhinocort liquid or Turbuhaler powder, Beconase, Nasalcort, etc. These medications usually bring allergic rhinitis under control when used once or twice daily.

Allergy shots are much more useful for treating the nose and eyes than for treating asthma. Conjunctivitis (eye inflammation) is a common sign of allergy to domestic pets, dust mites, or pollens. If antihistamine drops are put in the eyes the problem is often brought under control, but sometimes steroid drops may be needed. Also, repeated middle ear infections may be caused by rhinitis because the swelling can obstruct drainage through the fine channels (eustachian tubes) that extend from the middle ear to the nose. If this drainage is blocked, infection is common.

Many children with asthma also develop sinusitis, and if the infection is not well controlled by antibiotics, the sinusitis

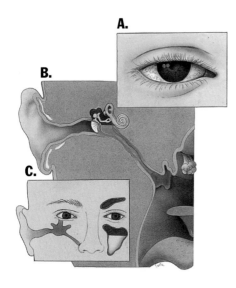

A.

B.

C.

Figure11–1. Ears, eyes, and sinuses. **A**, diagram of the eye , showing inflammation of the lining under the lids and over the eyeball.
B, diagram of the outer, middle, and inner ear. Note that the middle ear is drained by the eustachian tube, which empties into the back of the throat.
C, on the left side of the diagram, the eustachian tube is shown. On the right, fluid is shown in a sinus cavity.

can become chronic and can contribute to difficulty in controlling asthma. Associated postnasal drip from draining sinus fluid may cause persistent cough, especially at night.

CHAPTER TWELVE

EMOTIONS, DIET, AND ASTHMA

Asthma used to be considered a stress-related disease because in poorly controlled asthma, the hyperventilation associated with anxiety or anger may cause bronchospasm (due to drying of the airway lining). With good asthma control, even marked emotional stress is not likely to trigger an attack.

Much uncertainty surrounds the topic of diet and asthma, and often confusing advice is given. True allergic reactions to food are uncommon, but when they do occur, they can be devastating. Some people develop anaphylaxis after eating small quantities of nuts or shellfish. Even kissing someone who has just eaten peanuts can trigger anaphylaxis in highly sensitive individuals. Typically an anaphylactic reaction starts with a tingling in the mouth and on the lips, a tight sensation in the throat, flushing, and swelling of the throat which can rapidly make breathing difficult. A widespread itchy rash (hives) may develop. There can be wheezing, chest tightness, fainting, and shock. This severe reaction comes on within minutes of eating the offending food and can even cause death unless the child is carrying epinephrine in the form of an auto-injectable syringe or a puffer. The epinephrine puffer should be inhaled 10, 15, or even 20 times in rapid succession until improvement begins to occur. Puffs can be repeated every 15 to 30 minutes as needed if symptoms recur. You should also take the child to the emergency department where antihistamines and steroid medications will usually be given intravenously.

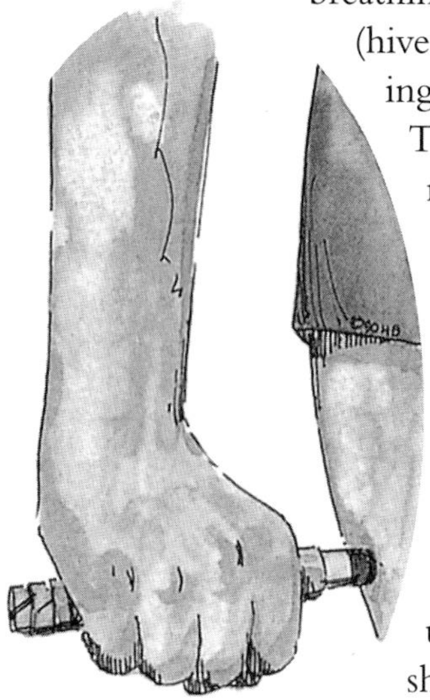

Figure 12–1.
Adrenaline (epinephrine)
injection using Med Epi Pen.

An allergic response to foods that comes on slowly is much more difficult to assess. Elimination diets (the elimination for about two weeks of one food after another) may help to decide whether certain foods such as dairy products or eggs are causing your child's problems. Unfortunately, skin tests for foods are not very useful in making this diagnosis. In children, moderate allergies to milk and eggs may disappear with time. It is worth trying a very small amount of the offending food again after 6 to 12 months to detect sensitivity to it.

Important: It is very important not to try foods that have already precipitated an anaphylactic reaction, since even a minute amount could cause life-threatening reactions or even death. Regrettably, all the ingredients in packaged foods are not always listed on the label. Children with anaphylaxis should learn to avoid foods not prepared at home, or only eat at the home of very close friends who are aware of the problem. Some artificial colorings, flavorings, and preservatives added to food can make asthma worse and these should be avoided. Check to see if food additives are listed on the product labels, and, if possible buy "preservative-free" foods. In Europe, these additives have been given numbers which must appear on the packages. Some of the most troublesome chemicals are sulfites and sulfur dioxide (E220, 221, 222, 226, 227). Sulfites and sulfur dioxide are used as preservatives in food and drink, particularly in beers and wines, in some salad bars, instant soups, synthetic orange drinks, and processed cooked meats (bologna or salami). See the list below:

1. **Tartrazine** (E102) is a yellow food color. It rarely causes asthma symptoms.
2. **Benzoic acid** (E210) is used as a preservative. It can be troublesome for asthmatics.
3. **ASA, salicylates** may occur naturally in some foods and can trigger asthma in 5 to 10% of people, usually in asso-

ciation with other symptoms such as fatigue, nasal polyps, mouth ulcers, and bowel disturbances. Foods such as yeast extract, mushrooms, and chocolate can contain salicylates.

4. **Monosodium glutamate** (MSG, E621) is used as a flavor enhancer in soy sauce, spices, stock cubes, potato chips, bacon, hamburgers, and packaged soups. Typical symptoms — sweating, flushing, tightness in the chest and fainting — are sometimes called the "Chinese restaurant syndrome." In asthmatics, wheezing may begin several hours after the meal.

SPECIAL DIETS

No known diets improve asthma, but there is some evidence that diets low in salt and animal fat, but high in fish oils, may improve asthma. If you have noticed that certain foods make your child's asthma worse, it is best to avoid them and to avoid food additives whenever possible.

CHAPTER THIRTEEN

ASTHMA TREATMENT CENTERS

Excellent asthma treatment centers for children and adults are located in most major cities, often in association with university hospitals. Asthma centers have the advantage of bringing together doctors who have a major interest in asthma, and patients who have the disease and require their help. These centers also do research, make available the latest treatments, and may ask you and your child to help with research projects to develop new treatments.

CONSULTATION WITH A SPECIALIST

If in spite of taking all the measures described in this book, your child continues to have problems, your doctor will often suggest a consultation with an asthma treatment specialist. Specialists see many different children with asthma, and this may help them develop a specific treatment plan for a child. The consultation usually consists of reviewing your child's medical history and physical examination, following which tests may be ordered. If your child is reasonably well at the time you see the specialist, only minor adjustments to the treatment program may be needed, but if your child is sick, major adjustments in treatment may be made or the specialist may suggest a short hospital stay to bring the asthma under control. At the treatment center, or in the hospital, you will usually begin an education program to improve your understanding of asthma and its treatment. This will help you become more confident with managing your child's asthma at home where you can start the treatment of flare-ups before they become severe. Reading material, videotapes, and specially trained asthma nurses or respiratory therapists may help to answer your questions. The asthma specialist, working with you and your family doctor, should be able to keep the asthma under good control.

ALTERNATIVE THERAPIES

You may have heard of "alternative" treatments. These treatments are not conventional and are often advertised with testimonials rather than scientific information. Testimonials always indicate that the treatment has been of great benefit and often feature individuals who say that they are much better than before. Practitioners providing alternative therapies always choose the best subjects they can in order to convince others to try their approach. Unfortunately, most of these "treatments" do not help, are often expensive, and are generally unscientific. Some of the alternative treatments have been tested in well-controlled clinical trials and have failed to show benefit. Initially, there may be some improvement because of the placebo effect (a combination of hope and suggestion), but over the long term, such treatments do not work. These "treatments" include hypnosis, acupuncture, homeopathy, chiropractic, and breathing exercises. Yoga and biofeedback may help some children to relax and avoid the panic that can accompany an asthma attack. Magnetic pads and negative ion generators have also been promoted without scientific basis. Surgery is of no value in treating asthma.

SELF-HELP GROUPS

These groups are often associated with an asthma center and can be helpful, especially for persons newly diagnosed with asthma. If you live far from a major city, you can contact these groups by mail, fax, or telephone. Printed material and videotapes are available through these organizations. By supporting your local lung association and other self-help organizations, financially and through volunteer work, you can help ensure that asthma research is pursued by doctors and scientists in order to develop better treatments and eventually a cure. A list of self-help organizations is provided on the inside front cover of this book.

CLINICAL ECOLOGY

Some people, including some doctors, think that asthma is caused by inhaling or eating tiny amounts of "harmful" substances. They have given this, and associated symptoms, names like "twentieth century disease" or "multiple environmental allergy syndrome." These doctors call themselves "clinical ecologists," although this is not a recognized medical specialty and has no scientific basis. It is dangerous (and expensive) to believe that asthma can be cured by avoiding household chemicals, being on a very strict diet, or even living in a specially constructed home or "bubble" with purified air. The diets can lead to severe malnutrition, and isolation can be emotionally harmful for children. The practitioners of this form of "treatment" play upon the gullibility of their patients. Fortunately, this "disease" and the treatments seem to be falling out of favor. But there will always be charlatans who will propose equally dangerous asthma treatments in the future. Such practices are particularly harmful if children who need asthma medications have them withdrawn in hopes of a miraculous cure. Bogus allergy tests are often linked to this form of medicine. Examples of this are analysis of a few hairs, measuring an increase in the pulse rate when children are given certain foods, or using the patient's tongue for allergy testing.

We recommend that if you choose to use an alternative therapy, the conventional treatment for asthma should also be continued, and you should let your asthma doctor know what you are doing so that they will be able to help if your child's asthma gets worse.

CHAPTER FOURTEEN

ASTHMA MANAGEMENT: THE NEAR AND DISTANT FUTURE

While cure of asthma is the ultimate goal of current research, it is unlikely that this goal will be reached soon. However, we know that most people with asthma can lead normal lives if they follow simple treatment principles. The best advice in the world is of no value unless it is *put into action consistently* by *you*. We encourage you to follow the instructions for asthma therapy given in this book.

NEW AND IMPROVED TREATMENTS

Since we now have a better understanding of how inflammation causes asthma, the emphasis of the pharmaceutical industry has been on developing better anti-inflammatory treatments with fewer side effects. In the United States (and other countries), the first people to benefit from new treatments are usually people cared for at university hospitals and teaching asthma centers where there is the opportunity to participate in research studies.

NEW BRONCHODILATORS

Two new bronchodilators — salmeterol or Serevent, and formoterol (which is not yet available in the USA) — are beta agonists that act for 12 hours or more, but otherwise which are very similar to albuterol/salbutamol (Proventil, Ventolin). Their main use is to improve asthma control in children who continue to have problems on high doses of inhaled steroid. They usually prevent waking up at night or chest tightness first thing in the morning. These medications may provide all-day relief from cold air or exercise-related breathlessness. Recently, it has been suggested that after using these medications for months, the beneficial effect may decrease somewhat. Salmeterol and formoterol should *never* be used as a substitute for inhaled steroids because they do not reduce inflammation. As salmeterol takes about 30 minutes to begin acting, it should not be used if you need to treat an attack quickly. Medications like salbuterol should be used in doses large enough to rescue the child from the attack. Formoterol begins to act within a few minutes and could be used to treat a severe asthma attack; however, because it is long acting, side effects will also persist. Thus, it may still be better to use shorter-acting bronchodilators (e.g., Proventil) for acute asthma attacks.

In children with asthma who need large doses of inhaled steroids (over 1000 mcg of beclomethasone or equivalent), salmeterol has been shown to have a steroid-sparing effect that allows high doses to be reduced to more acceptable levels.

BLOCKERS OF NATURAL CHEMICAL MEDIATORS

In recent years, asthma research has shown that inflammation is due to the release of a great number of chemicals from the immune cells in the body. These chemicals, called mediators, normally fight viruses, bacteria, and parasites and help cells to communicate with each other. In asthma, they may be released in excess amounts, and inflammation is increased out of control, causing narrowing of the airways and excess secretions. Blockers of some of these mediators may help to control some aspects of the asthma response. The first of these, an LTD_4 antagonist has recently become available and others will doubtless follow soon.

STEROIDS

The steroids currently available provide excellent control for most children, if used regularly. They also cause few side effects, and the greater beneficial effects can be further enhanced by inhaling the steroid from an MDI and a holding chamber. It is likely that improved accessory devices will be available for use with the newer CFC-free metered dose inhalers that deliver aerosol on breathing in. Another approach is to use powder inhalers, which will probably improve over the next few years and function more like puffers. Except for the delivery of new medications, these devices will probably replace nebulizers. More potent and even safer inhaled steroids that require only a small number of puffs, two or three times a day, have recently become available in the United States. An example of this is Flovent available in puffers of 25, 50, 125, 250 mcg per puff in Canada, 44, 110 in the UK, and 44, 110, and 220 mcg per puff in the USA.

ASTHMA MONITORING

It is likely that more asthmatics will monitor their asthma with a peak flow meter or a portable spirometer. This will make it easier to ensure that the treatment not only relieves the symptoms, but also preserves lung function. Having the medication to deal with asthma and a method to monitor asthma control will empower older children (or parents of younger children) to undertake care of the disorder themselves most of the time, just as people with high blood pressure or diabetes do. It is important to remember that excellent asthma control should also prevent long-term damage to the air passages.

IMMUNOTHERAPY

Allergy shots are likely to be used less frequently because in asthma, unlike in rhinitis, this treatment is not very effective and can have unpleasant side effects. Immunotherapy is also expensive, time consuming, and painful. Many allergy specialists no longer use allergy shots to treat asthma.

THEOPHYLLINE

Theophylline is used much less frequently than it used to be and may gradually be discontinued as better aerosol treatments are introduced. The tablets are less potent than bronchodilator MDIs, act only for the same length of time as the longer acting aerosols, and can cause serious side effects. There is ongoing research to develop a form of theophylline with greater beneficial effects and fewer side effects.

ANTIHISTAMINES, INCLUDING KETOTIFEN

Antihistamines are currently used for treating nasal allergies. They have not been very effective in treating asthma because histamine is not one of the more important mediators underlying airway inflammation. It is not likely that these medications will have an important role to play in future asthma treatment.

CURING ASTHMA: THE ULTIMATE GOAL

A cure for asthma is the goal of today's research. We hope that with increasing knowledge, persistence, and new approaches, a cure may be found. Even today, without a cure, asthma can be well controlled in nearly all the children. By working closely with your doctor it should be possible to conquer childhood asthma.

CHAPTER FIFTEEN

ANSWERS TO COMMON QUESTIONS

Q. Will my child grow out of the asthma?

A. About half of children with asthma "grow out" of it when they are teenagers, although it may return in later years, especially if the person starts smoking. Some children continue to have asthma as adults. Adults who have asthma do not grow out of it, although there will be times when symptoms are more or less troublesome.

Q. Can asthma be cured?

A. At this time, there is no cure for asthma. However, eliminating specific allergens (such as exposure to a cat) may allow you to discontinue some, or even all, medications. Available treatments can usually completely control asthma symptoms, if they are taken properly.

Q. Will exercise help?

A. Exercise is one of the triggers that can bring on asthma, and this may discourage children with asthma from taking part in sports. Proper treatment allows children with asthma to exercise normally. Good physical fitness will, in turn, make it easier to breathe at all times.

Q. Do breathing exercises help?

A. Breathing exercises are special ways of breathing in and out slowly. The idea is that this will "strengthen the lungs." No scientific evidence is available to support that breathing exercises specifically help asthma, although learning how to control breathing and reduce panic can be useful during asthma attacks.

Q. Should we try an ionizer?

A. There are several ionizers on the market that are claimed to help asthma. These machines are meant to create negatively-charged particles (ions), but there is no evidence either that negative ions are useful for treating asthma or that ionizers benefit anybody but the company selling them.

Q. Should my child go on a special diet?

A. Little is known about the influence of diet on asthma. Sometimes, certain foods seem to cause asthma symptoms to worsen. For example, some people develop wheezing after eating nuts, shellfish, or strawberries, and this may be associated with swelling and tingling of the lips and tongue or an itchy skin rash. This is part of a generalized allergic reaction (*anaphylaxis*) that could be life threatening. People who have this type of response after eating these foods should avoid them. If you do not have this type of response, avoiding these foods will not help your asthma. Some common foods (such as potatoes, celery, dairy products, or eggs) may cause worsening of asthma in some people. If you think that your asthma is worse after eating a certain type of food, try avoiding it for several weeks and see whether this helps. Some children with asthma have increased symptoms because of food additives. The most common troublesome additive is metabisulfite, which is used as a preservative in certain drinks (including beer and wine). Symptoms usually develop immediately after consuming the metabisulfite. The best policy is avoidance. Although there are certain strange diets that may be recommended to people with asthma, no scientific basis exists for their use.

Q. Does eating natural food or health food help?

A. There is no reason to suppose that eating organically grown vegetables or health food is of particular benefit in asthma, and there is no evidence to prove that chemical fertilizers used in the growing of fruit and vegetables cause problems in asthma.

Q. Are there any precautions to take when going on vacation?

A. It is important to take supplies of your asthma treatment, including any treatment you would normally use for severe attacks (such as oral steroids). This is particularly important when you go to another country, because the same treatments may not be available there. You should always take a list of your treatments (with the generic name of the drugs). It is safe to have the normal vaccinations required for some countries and to take antimalarial tablets as these will not worsen asthma. It is also safe to fly in a pressurized aircraft. Again, make sure you always take your treatment with you since airplanes rarely have on board emergency treatment for asthma.

Q. Will I pass asthma on to my children?

A. Asthma and other allergic diseases such as rhinitis ("hay fever") tend to run in families, so that children with a strong family history of allergic disorders are more likely to inherit them. However, even if both parents have allergies or asthma, this does not necessarily mean that their children will develop these problems.

Q. Is asthma all in the mind?

A. Asthma is never "all in the mind." Asthma is an inflammatory condition of the airways caused by a genetic predisposition in combination with certain asthma triggers in the environment. Nevertheless, most asthmatics notice that their asthma tends to be worse when they are under considerable emotional stress. With treatment, the asthma can be so well controlled that even major stressful episodes should have little, or no, effect. A condition known as pseudo-asthma or psychogenic wheezing exists, but this condition is relatively uncommon (see page 80).

Q. Should we move to another house and would a change of climate help?
A. Changing the place where you live is unlikely to be helpful in the long term. For example, there is little point in moving to Arizona where communities have turned deserts into lawns and floral gardens. On the other hand, if you are allergic to domestic pets or house dust mites, removing these from your environment will certainly result in marked improvement in the allergic complaints just as completely removing tobacco smoke is likely to help.

Q. Should we get rid of the pets?
A. If your pet is a trigger for your child's asthma, you would be wise to eliminate the cause. However, your pet may not be the cause of your child's asthma. Allergy skin tests can be used to determine whether the pet may be causing the problem. The best way to find out if you should give away your pet is to see if symptoms improve while you are away from home for several weeks on vacation. If you have an allergic child with asthma, it is not a good idea to go out and buy a furry pet on the off chance that allergies to the pet will not develop. Children can become allergically sensitized to pets after a time, and if the pet remains in the house, this can be a constant inflammatory allergic trigger that makes asthma more difficult to manage. Just because you have always had a pet, and your child's asthma only developed recently, this does not mean that he or she is not allergic to the animal. Allergies can develop equally to pets with long or short hair, since it is the dander and not the hair that produces the allergic reaction. Similarly, there are no breeds of dog or cat that are "good" for asthma although we have heard myths about certain breeds (chihuahua, for example) not producing allergies. This is not true.

Q. Could my child die of an asthma attack?

A. Occasionally, people with asthma do die. However, death from asthma is rare and almost never occurs if the asthma is properly treated. Those who die of asthma usually have not monitored their asthma and kept it under good control. Asthma usually tends to get worse over several days before it becomes life threatening. If oral steroids do not produce improvement within four hours, or if your child is getting worse quickly, you should go to the nearest hospital emergency department at once.

Q. Should my child have the influenza shot?

A. Yes. The influenza immunization should be given every year in the fall before the beginning of each "flu" season except to people who are documented to be allergic to eggs. This is because people with asthma are at high risk of serious flare-ups if they get influenza. The flu shot must be given each year because the flu virus changes each year. The flu shot, however, will *not* protect your child from viral colds or pneumonia.

Q. Will asthma give my child lung cancer?

A. No. There is absolutely no connection between asthma and lung cancer. Smoking is the main cause of lung cancer, and asthmatics should never smoke or be exposed to second-hand smoke.

Q. Will asthma cause permanent damage to my child's lungs?

A. Rarely. The only times the lungs are damaged are if there is another chest problem along with asthma or if persistent airway inflammation goes untreated. Asthma may cause chronic changes in your lungs similar to emphysema after you have had it for a long time, but this occurs mainly in people who smoke. You can help to avoid permanent injury by keeping the asthma well controlled at all times and by immediately treating asthma attacks.

Q. Will asthma have a harmful effect on my child's heart or lead to heart attacks?
A. No. Asthma will not affect the heart if it is well controlled. Severe asthma attacks leading to low levels of oxygen in the blood may cause heart problems, but this is secondary to the breathing difficulty.

Q. Can people with asthma travel by airplane?
A. Yes, as long as the asthma is *under control*, and they have their bronchodilator inhalers with them on the airplane and not in their checked-in luggage.

Q. Can my child become "addicted" to asthma inhalers?
A. No. Using asthma inhalers regularly to control the disease does not make you "dependent" on them. Taking your anti-inflammatory preventer medicines regularly in adequate doses should control the inflammation, making it much less necessary to use bronchodilators.

APPENDIX 1

AVOIDING ATMOSPHERIC POLLEN AND MOLD SPORES

You may be allergic to the following:
- Tree pollen, occurring between March and early June
- Grass pollen, occurring between early May and the end of July
- Ragweed pollen, occurring between early August and the end of September or the first killing frost
- Mold spores, occurring throughout the summer, especially between July and October.

You can reduce your exposure to these particles in the allergy season by

1. *Keeping windows and doors closed to prevent the particles from entering your home.* An air-conditioner will help in hot weather. Be sure that the air-conditioner and furnace filters are cleaned regularly.
2. *Avoiding being outdoors when the counts are highest,* i.e., on sunny days in the morning and afternoon. The counts are lowest immediately after rain, in the evening, and at night.
3. *Avoiding high exposure.* Exposure to pollen and mold spores is increased by cutting grass, camping, and going into barns. Exposure to mold spores is also increased by sweeping up leaves and working with compost heaps. It is also important to reduce molds by decreasing the humidity in places like your basement.
4. *Taking a holiday out of allergy season or to an area with low counts.* The latter is practical only for ragweed pollen, which is mainly localized to central and east North America. Booklets are available that give the index of the level of ragweed pollen counts.

5. If you use a home humidifier, add an anti-mold solution to the water (available in drug and appliance stores). In general, humidifiers are not recommended for children with asthma as high humidity can increase the amount of mold and dust mites.

AVOIDING ANIMALS AND BIRDS

Allergy to animals and birds often causes more trouble in winter months because the house is closed up, the pet is indoors more, and you are also indoors more.

1. If there is allergy to a pet, it should be removed from the home.
2. If you are not willing to remove the pet, you can reduce exposure
    - by keeping the pet outdoors as much as possible.
    - by *never* allowing the pet in the bedroom.
    - by only allowing the pet to enter certain rooms and by keeping it off furniture, which tends to collect allergens.
    - by washing and brushing the pet frequently (every 2 to 4 weeks) — not by the asthmatic person.
    - by having another family member feed and care for the pet. Remember that clothes worn by that person will have allergens on them.
3. Medicines are available that can be taken to relieve or prevent symptoms of asthma, rhinitis, or conjunctivitis. These may be useful when you do not keep a pet yourself, but will be exposed to one when visiting the home of friends. In this situation, also ask if the pet can be kept out of the room you are in.

The extent to which a pet is making symptoms worse can be tested by a trial period of 3 or 4 months, during which the pet is removed from the home (and the home is thoroughly cleaned and ventilated), or during which you are away from home.

DUST CONTROL FOR HOUSE DUST MITE ALLERGY

1. Pillows and mattress should be encased in zippered vinyl or a new "breathing" Gortex-like material (not needed with waterbeds). This mattress and pillow covering can be purchased from [Allergy Control Products Inc., 96 Danbury Road, Ridgefield, CT 06877 1-800-422-DUST]. Alternatively, use fiberfill pillows, and wash them monthly on the hot cycle and then dry thoroughly. The mattress should be vacuumed twice weekly by someone other than the allergic person. Foam, kapok, or feather pillows collect dust — do not use them. Do not use wool blankets or sheepskin pads.

2. Do not use vaporizers or humidifiers in the bedroom — house humidity over 30 to 40% allows house dust mites to thrive! Add anti-mold solutions to floor-type humidifiers used elsewhere.

3. Keep pets out of the bedroom and other areas used frequently by the allergic person.

4. Keep dust-catching carpets, blinds, drapes, armchairs to a minimum or remove them. Shades are the easiest window covering to keep clean and blinds the most difficult. Keep stuffed animals out of the child's bed.

5. If heating with hot air, seal the vents and use an alternative heater in the bedroom or filter the dust by covering the bedroom vents with furnace filter material. Wash or replace the furnace filter monthly.

6. Avoid keeping damp duster/mop in the bedroom.

7. Clean out drawers every three months.

8. The allergic person should be out of the house when vacuuming is done. Central vacuum systems are best. They exhaust dust to a specific collection spot.

9. Furnace or room air cleaners are of doubtful value and do not replace other control methods.
10. Avoid living in a basement apartment, if possible.

EXERCISE

Exercise is beneficial for everyone. If you are fit, you will be able to do more work. People with chest disease often avoid exercise, although exercise is beneficial to them. Exercise strengthens the heart and body muscles, makes better use of oxygen, and generally improves the sense of well-being.

If you are short of breath when you exercise, keep these points in mind:

1. Each person is capable of different amounts of exercise depending on the severity of their problem and their level of fitness.
2. Daily activities around the house do not provide enough exercise. You need to do something more strenuous and continuous.
3. Start with easy activities such as walking on a level for 10 minutes twice a day, increasing to 30 minutes twice a day. Then add more strenuous activities such as walking uphill, cycling, or jogging.
4. Exercise should be done daily. It does not have to be exhausting to improve fitness. In fact, regular exercise such as walking is more beneficial than occasional stress-ful exercise like running. A brisk walk of 3 kilometers (2 miles) daily will keep you reasonably fit. This should not take more than 15 to 30 minutes.
5. Exercise indoors when the weather is cold or damp and when air pollution counts are high, if these factors bother you. Using a stationary bicycle or stair stepping provides good indoor exercise.

6. If exercise worsens your asthma, use an inhaled bron-chodilator at least 10 minutes before you start to exercise.

THE SEVEN RULES OF ASTHMA THERAPY

1. KNOW YOUR ASTHMA

Learn to recognize when your child's asthma is getting out of control so that you can treat it early. Sometimes the symptoms will tell you that your child is getting worse, while at other times the clue may be that more bronchodilator puffs than usual are needed. To avoid your child getting into serious difficulty without advance warning, regularly measure the peak flow, as this can alert you to the need to increase the preventer medications.

2. KNOW YOUR TRIGGERS AND AVOID THEM

Asthma triggers might include allergens such as cats, house dust mites, and pollens and irritants like tobacco smoke, fumes, and volatile chemicals. Reduce exposure to them with careful environmental control and thus minimize the need for medications. It is better to clean up the home to prevent an attack than to try to clean up an asthma attack with medications after it has started.

3. DON'T TEMPT FATE

For example, people with asthma should not acquire new pets thinking that they will not become allergic to them. It is also important to get the influenza immunization each year rather than risk getting the "flu." It is not wise to stop asthma medications too soon just because your child seems to be feeling well and you think the asthma *might* not come back.

4. KNOW YOUR MEDICATIONS

You should know not only the name and dose of each medication but also its expected benefits and side effects. You should also calculate how long each inhaler should last so that your child does not end up taking puffs from an inhaler that no longer contains active medication. Have spare medication available in each place where your and your child will be staying — such as school or different homes where you visit.

5. TAKE PRESCRIBED PREVENTER (ANTI–INFLAMMATORY) MEDICATIONS REGULARLY

Preventer medications do not open up airways like bronchodilators can, but they are the most important of the medications that your child takes because, when used regularly, they reduce asthmatic inflammation. The best time to treat an asthma attack is the day before it happens.

6. KNOW WHEN AND HOW TO USE RELIEVER MEDICATIONS

Consistently follow the asthma care plan developed with your doctor. It is better to use less medication too early than a lot of bronchodilator too late.

7. LEARN AS MUCH AS YOU CAN ABOUT ASTHMA

Ask questions, read books, arrange regular follow-up visits with your doctor to make sure that your child's asthma remains under control and take advantage of new treatments as they become available. Get involved in an asthma care organization such as your local Lung Association.